Anonymous

Alfred in India

Or, Scenes in Hindoostan

Anonymous

Alfred in India
Or, Scenes in Hindoostan

ISBN/EAN: 9783337058913

Printed in Europe, USA, Canada, Australia, Japan

Cover: Foto ©Andreas Hilbeck / pixelio.de

More available books at **www.hansebooks.com**

ALFRED IN INDIA

OR

SCENES IN HINDOOSTAN

WILLIAM AND ROBERT CHAMBERS

LONDON AND EDINBURGH

1869.

Edinburgh:
Printed by W. and R. Chambers.

The present volume consists of a familiar account of the more interesting features of English life in India, with a view to the amusement and instruction of young people. It has been written by a lady who has returned to England with her family from India; and the style aimed at is such as has been approved of in Miss Edgeworth's " Frank," and similar productions.

ALFRED IN INDIA.

INTRODUCTORY.

Young persons often hear of INDIA; they are told of relations who are in INDIA, and they see a number of things which are said to come from INDIA. Where is this India, in which the people of Great Britain are so much interested? India —or Hindoostan, as it is otherwise called—is a country of vast size in Asia; and on looking at a terrestrial globe, we see that it is at the opposite side of the earth from us, and at least eight thousand miles from England.

It would be a long story to tell how the English acquired a settlement in India, and made themselves masters of the country. About two hundred years ago, a society of English merchants, called the East India Company, began to trade with the natives of India; and partly at the solicitation of the native princes, and partly for self-defence, they, from less to more, found themselves under the necessity of assuming the supreme authority. The East India Company, therefore, is the governing power in India; and it employs a large body of English in its service. It is for this purpose that so many persons go from England to India. For the better governing of the country, the Queen appoints a Governor-General, whose residence is at Calcutta, which is the capital of India. It is very fortunate for the Indians that their country has come under British rule, for they now live at peace, free from the capricious tyranny of native oppressors. But this can only be said of our own provinces, for there are still a number of independent states where the people are as badly off as ever.

The appearance of India—its people, customs, language, productions, almost everything—differs from what is seen or prevails in England. The very way in which the English live in India is quite different from the manner in which they live at home. And here we may remark, that the English in India, though living there many years, always speak of England as *home:* they consider India only to be a place of temporary abode, which they will some day leave, and go back to the land of their fathers. An important reason for their not wishing to reside permanently in India, is the nature of the climate, which does not agree with the health of the people of Great Britain. It is more especially dangerous to leave children in India at those early years when the constitution is forming. They are always sent home, not only for their education, but that they may grow up healthy and strong. The year is divided into three seasons—the rainy, the cold, and the hot. The rainy in general extends from June till October; the cold from November till February; the hot from March till May. The rainy season is unhealthy; and the hot, in some districts, is scarcely endurable. To accommodate themselves as far as possible to the dreadfully sultry weather, the English wear light cotton dresses, and seldom move out of doors, except in the morning and evening. But about this something will be afterwards related.

Much of India is in a wild state, partially

covered with bushes, called jungle; but large districts are cultivated, as fields of rice, indigo, and other products, by the natives. The native population consists chiefly of two distinct races —Hindoos and Mohammedans. By far the greater number are Hindoos, who are a very ancient people, industrious, gentle in manners, and possess various other good qualities; but they labour under some grievous errors of opinion, which greatly retard their improvement. Their religion, called Brahminism, is a gross superstition; for it makes them worship images, and also many things besides, at which a child in England would be inclined to laugh. It is part of their religion to divide themselves into *castes*. A caste is a class, and the persons who belong to one class cannot associate or eat with those of another. Each class, also, has its own trades, and its members dare not follow the profession of another class. All this is very bad, and must keep the Hindoos in a low state of civilisation. The natives, however, know no better, and are contented. They are for the most part disposed to live at peace, and to serve the English. Their wants, also, are few; their dress is light and cheap; they can live on a little rice; and their houses, which are easily erected, have no expensive furniture. In fact they live in the open air, where they eat, entertain their friends, and transact their business, using their houses merely as places to sleep in. In various quarters there are English missionaries and teachers; and many Hindoo children learn to read and speak English. The Hindoos chiefly inhabit the lower provinces, and are darker in complexion, and more feeble, than the inhabitants of the upper or northern provinces, who are mostly Mohammedans.

The northern parts of India are bounded by the Himaleh Mountains. These are very lofty, and their summits are perpetually covered with snow. From these high mountains descend many streams; the larger rivers being the Indus on the west, and the Ganges in the north and east; the latter being considered a sacred river by the Hindoos. The low-lying district through which the Ganges flows, before entering the sea, is called Bengal, a country rich, populous, and productive. There are some large cities in India besides Calcutta; their names are—Delhi, Benares, Agra, Patnah, Moorshedabad, Dacca, Madras, and Bombay. The things which appear remarkable to an Englishman arriving in India, are the dingy-coloured natives in their fanciful dresses; the luxuriant vegetation; the burning sun overhead; and the strange animals, beasts, birds, and reptiles. The variety of languages is likewise strange. Hindoostanee is the dialect most generally used, more especially by the Mohammedans, and the officers of government and the military; while Bengalee is spoken by many of the Hindoos. Persons going to reside in India require to learn at least Hindoostanee; and some, besides, study Persic, Arabic, and Sanscrit—the learned languages. Many of the poorer classes in Calcutta speak English; but in all the provinces the domestic servants speak Hindoostanee.

Although the English have now been long in the country, they do not exchange visits with natives even of rank and good education, except on occasions of ceremony; the unhappy division into castes, and prejudices as to food, causing the natives to shun familiar contact with Europeans. Where a man believes that he would be polluted by eating in company with a person of a different religion or caste, he can never be on social terms with strangers. The dwellings of the poorer natives are chiefly huts made of frames of bamboo, covered with reed matting, with thatched or tiled roofs; the floors are of mud; a few very rude couches are around; the few cooking utensils are of earthenware, with a single brass vessel, as a sign of comparative wealth; and a stool perhaps completes the articles of furniture. A European is never allowed to enter their dwellings, as his presence would be believed to pollute them. Plenty of naked children, not very clean, are observed playing about the doors; but unless of the very lowest rank, their mothers are never to be seen. They are employed in preparing the food, or in grinding the different grains with small handmills: a wife never eats with her husband, but waits till he has done, which seems to us a lamentable degradation.

The dress of the natives is mostly cotton cloth, with a turban of the same material on the head. The lower parts of the legs and feet of the poorer classes are generally bare. All wear a sash of some kind, called a *cumberbund*, which is of muslin or silk, and worn in many folds. Rich natives use handsome shawls for this purpose. It is considered a mark of disrespect to appear without a cumberbund.

The Great Mogul, as he was formerly called—the descendant of the Mohammedan conquerors of India—lives in Delhi, on a moderate stipend allowed him by the British. But although imperial rule is completely at an end, no attempt has been made to interfere with the ancient institutions of the people. The most remarkable of these institutions is called the "Village-system," which still intersects India almost like a network, every mesh of the net being a little separate self-governed territory, with its own town, its own community, and all the materials of a state within itself.

India has long been noted for the richness of its productions. Rice and indigo, with wheat in the upper provinces, are raised in great abundance, besides an immense variety of fruits and vegetables. In the north, cotton and sugar are cultivated, and wheat and almost all European plants thrive. Among the more remarkable trees may be mentioned the bamboo, which is properly a tall grass, but each blade is a gigantic cane, sometimes reaching to the height of a hundred feet. It is not unfrequently two feet in circumference at the thickest part; and in this case pails or buckets are made of its joints. Then there is mahogany, little inferior to that of Honduras; teak, used for ship-building; and a host of other trees. Almost all European fruit-trees succeed as well as in their own countries; but the native mangoe is common all over India. The fruit is of an oblong shape, from two to six inches in length; the flavour is very delicious. A cluster of mangoe-trees is called a *mangoe tope*. These groves are planted by good people in India from the same motives that the charitable in England endow hospitals. They think their souls will be benefited by the blessings of the weary travellers who rest in the shade of their trees, and refresh themselves with their fruit. Innumerable tanks and wells are constructed with the same view; and whole towns and villages are imbedded, as it were, in mangoe, tamarind, and peepul-trees, planted for the good of strangers perhaps then unborn. The silkworm has for ages furnished great quantities of silk, which the natives have dressed, and dyed, and woven into shawls, handkerchiefs, and other articles. But the manufacture of silk, and also of cotton, is now as well, if not better, executed in England; and much cheaper, in consequence of our superior machinery, which the poor but ingenious natives of India do not understand, and cannot afford to buy. Cotton and silk, in a raw state, wool, opium, indigo, sugar, saltpetre, rice, and pepper, are the chief éxports; and the imports from Britain consist of every variety of manufactured articles. India is considered to be one of the best customers of England; the trade employs a great number of ships.

India possesses a variety of animals, which are found in no other part of the world. The largest and most remarkable of these is the elephant, specimens of which are brought to England, and shown in menageries and zoological gardens. The tiger, a very ferocious creature, is found in the marshy jungles in various parts of the country. India abounds in monkeys, and has some peculiar races of dogs. When English dogs are taken to India, they do not thrive, the climate being too warm for them. There are various kinds of oxen, among which are the white bull and cow: these are held in great reverence by the natives. There are many splendid kinds of birds—as shining creepers, parrots, paroquets, lories, cockatoos, and other highly-coloured feathered animals. There are likewise vultures, bustards, peacocks, and nearly all kinds of game birds and poultry of Britain. On arriving at Calcutta, a stranger will be amused at seeing great numbers of birds called adjutants. These are tall and large creatures, with a very long and powerful bill. They are often seen standing on one leg, as if pensive and thoughtful, and they are so tame, that they walk about among the people without any fear. Some of them are from five to six feet high. In Indian towns, these adjutant birds are extremely useful in devouring and clearing away all sorts of offal; so that they may be called a kind of scavengers or street-cleaners. Throughout India there are many reptiles, as crocodiles, lizards, and serpents or snakes, some of which are dangerous. India has also many remarkable insects, one of which, the kermes, produces a fine scarlet dye. The mosquito is very troublesome in some quarters of the country. Fish, of an immense number of varieties, abound in all the streams and waters, and are frequently of exceeding brilliancy of colour.

The English who go to India are chiefly in

government employments, for the most part connected with the army; but there are also numbers in the civil service, and they reside at what are called *stations*. These are places where military are stationed, and some of them are many hundreds of miles up the country. The mode of living at these stations, and how children amuse themselves at them, will be described in the pages which follow.

Sometimes it is found necessary to make a station for a regiment or a magistrate where there was not even a village before; there are also large native towns without any Company's servant residing there, and of course they are not called stations. It is a great pleasure, after a long and fatiguing journey, to come all at once in sight of the huts of the natives, and the white houses and bungalows of the Europeans, with their green Venetian blinds, each looking so pretty in its separate lawn, or *compound*, as the enclosures are termed. There is a considerable distinction between a *house* in India and a *bungalow*. What is called a house has always a flat roof, which makes a fine terrace to walk on. Houses are sometimes one storey, sometimes two or three storeys high. All the houses in Calcutta in which Europeans live are *houses;* but in small stations the dwellings are generally *bungalows.* The natives either live in a hut, little better than a shed, or in a house; for they take great pleasure in sitting on the terraces of their roofs early in the morning or late in the evening: they could not do this on a bungalow roof; and the heat of a house is not so much an objection to them as to a European.

The bungalow is a habitation suitable to the climate of India. It may be described as a kind of cottage, with a sloping thatched roof, and all the rooms are on the ground-floor. There are generally some steps outside the house, but none inside. In the middle of the bungalow is a large hall or room, with doors all round it, which open into smaller rooms, which are the sleeping apartments; and generally all round these smaller rooms is an open veranda or colonnade, part of which, at the corners, is enclosed for baths. There are no windows in the middle room, the light comes in through the doors; the exclusion of heat being a most important object in the construction of the dwelling. The ceiling of the room is usually composed of cotton cloth, whitewashed and stretched on a bamboo framework. The front is used as a kind of lobby, where the servants sit, and the tailors work, and the children run about and play. In no bungalow is there any kitchen: the cooking is performed in a separate building at some distance. Neither are there any apartments for the servants, who are all natives, with very simple wants. At night, these useful and humble beings spread their mats on the floors of any of the verandas, roll themselves round and round in a sheet, put a little hard pillow under their heads, and are asleep in a moment.

During that part of the day when the sun is most powerful, the family sit in the darkened central room of the bungalow, and are glad to procure cool draughts of air by the waving of a *punkah*. A punkah is a large oblong fan suspended by cords from the roof, and it is drawn to and fro with a rope by the servants. By the swinging of the machine the air is agitated; there is a great wind—so great, that every light thing on the table requires to be kept in its place by a weight. This agitation of the air is exceedingly refreshing; and should the poor bearer fall asleep, or cease to pull, the heat becomes intolerable. The punkah, in short, is an indispensable piece of furniture in every bungalow. In certain seasons, it requires to be pulled not only all day, but all night; and as the doorways into the bedrooms from the central apartment are provided only with silk screens, the air from the punkah is allowed to enter and refresh the sleepers. Besides the large punkahs, there are smaller fans called *hand-punkahs*, which sometimes require to be employed. To aid in cooling the bungalow while the hot wind blows in April, May, and part of June, mats made of a sweet smelling grass are hung up at the western door; they are kept constantly wet, and the air is cooled by the evaporation which takes place. These mats are called *tatties*.

With all the means that are adopted to subdue the oppressive heat, the health of the English would sink unless they frequently bathed. Water is brought to the bungalow by a servant who is called a *bhestie*. This man is never idle. He carries water in a bag made of a skin, which is slung over his back, and his duty is to water the tatties, and bring water for the baths. Some persons bathe merely by having a bagful of water thrown over them. This is very refreshing and invigorating. The servant who takes charge of the water for drinking is called an *aubdar;* rain-water is generally preferred for drinking, and is collected in the rainy season in large sheets fastened to four poles, and carefully preserved in large earthen jars about four feet high.

In the bungalows there are no floors to scour, for they are not wooden, but a composition of lime and other materials, beaten as hard as stone; and these are always covered with mats, which are brushed clean twice every day by a man called a *mehter*, or sweeper. The bearers clean the furniture, and generally arrange the beds. There are no feather-beds to shake up, so that it is a much easier operation than in England. All the servants are men—cooks, apartment cleaners, attendants, and washers of the family linen. The clothes-washer is called a *dhobie*. He takes the articles on his ass to some convenient spot on the banks of a river, or if he is not near a river, to some artificial pond, or, as it is called in India, *tank;* and there, instead of washing the linen with his hands, as the maids do here, he beats it with all his might on hard wooden slabs till it is clean, and then bleaches and dries it in the sun. This does not take long; and then he reloads his ass, and takes the clothes to his house to iron. The person who waits at table is called a *kitmutgar*, and the man who would be called a butler here is called a *khansaman;* but he not only attends to the table, but goes to market, and takes a sort of charge of all the servants, particularly the cook.

Ordinary labourers, or men who are hired to do some work, are called *coolies;* they usually carry their burdens on their head. The *chaprassey* is a person who is employed to go on messages, to attend on ladies when they go out, and to perform all the duties of a footman, except waiting at table. The chaprasseys also act as a kind of policemen when in the service of the Company's officers. The *syce* is a man who attends on horses; each horse requires one of these grooms, besides a man to cut grass for it daily. *Chokeydar* is the name given to a watchman.

In India many servants are required, for in general each does only one thing. Thus the kitmutgars only wait at table, and each person in the family has one for himself. The servant who announces visitors, or goes on messages, usually sits in the entrance or lobby, or, as it is called in India, the *veranda*, to be ready when he is required; and when he hears his master or mistress say, "Qui hi?" which means, "Who waits?" he comes immediately, just as the servants here do when they hear the bell ring.

The bearers are the most generally useful, for besides carrying the palanquins, they pull the punkahs, and perform some other useful services. There are seldom fewer than five bearers in each house, and sometimes as many as eight, or even more. The needlework of the family is done by a *durzie*, or tailor, who sits in the lobby or veranda all day on a mat, and works away: he does not sew very quickly, but so neatly, that no woman could do it better. The only women-servants ever employed are the *ayahs*, or ladies'-maids, who take care of very young children. Most of the ayahs can sew a little, but only sufficient to make their own clothes.

The servants have small houses of their own in the compound, but they do not cook and eat their food together. Some are Hindoos, and some Mohammedans, and they will not eat with each other; and both sects think, with the Pharisees of old, that they are more or less holy according to what they eat or drink, or with whom they eat or drink. They will not eat food that has been touched by a European, or by one of lower caste than themselves. One bearer cooks for the rest of his brothers, as they call each other; and the kitmutgars do the same; and so on with the rest. They are always talking about their food, and seem to think of little else; but they only take two meals in the day—one early in the forenoon, and one after sunset. The servants do not mind touching and serving food to the families of their employers, though they will eat no part of that food themselves. Besides the usual meals of breakfast and dinner, the English in India take luncheon, which is called *tiffin*.

Europeans in India do not (except in Ceylon) travel by coaches as in England, because there are few made roads on which carriages with wheels could go. Travelling is performed chiefly by *palanquins*, which are a kind of covered couches carried on poles. The carrying, however, is fatiguing to the bearers, and to travel any considerable distance, relays of fresh bearers must be provided. To travel *dâk*, is to go by palanquins, for which fresh bearers are ready at every stage—this is like posting in England. The dâk is under government control, and in the post-office department. The expense, usually at the rate of eight annas per mile for an entire set of twelve men, is paid beforehand. The average length of the stage is ten miles, which occupy about three hours; and at the end of each stage a gratuity is given to the runners, as in English posting.

A palanquin in which the traveller does not recline, but sits up, is called a *tanjahn*, and is used for short distances. The grandest method of travelling is on the back of an elephant; but this is practised chiefly in the jungle. The elephant is also of great use in carrying baggage. When to be employed for riding, he kneels, and by means of a ladder, it is easy to mount on his back, on which an ornamented seat, called a *houdah*, is fixed. The houdah will hold two persons. The elephant does not require any bridle: a driver, called a *mahout*, sits on his neck, and urges him forward with a sharp-pointed stick. The elephant, however, is very tractable, and a word will make him kneel, or rise, or stop, or go forward. Distance, in travelling, is measured by *coss;* a coss is equal to about two miles.

In walking out, and also sometimes in riding, it is necessary to have a *chattah,* or umbrella, over the head, to avert the rays of the sun. Very large chattahs are carried in India by the bearers over the heads of their masters and mistresses.

The money used in India consists of pice, annas, and rupees. Four pice make one anna, and sixteen annas make one rupee. A rupee is a silver coin worth two shillings; consequently an anna is equal to three-halfpence.

THE MEHLA.

Alfred and Charles were two little boys who were born in India, and lived with their father and mother in a retired station at a certain distance from the great city of Patnah.

There were very few Europeans at the same place, and the little boys were the constant companions of their parents, who tried by every means in their power to make up for the want of those advantages which children in Britain enjoy. Alfred and Charles profited by what they were taught; and though there was no school for them to attend daily, and new books were very seldom to be had, their kind father and mother contrived to find employment and amusement for them during the long hot day, from sunrise to sunset. Though their manner of life was in some respects different from that of little boys and girls in this country, there are no wonderful adventures to be related of them. The only separation the children had ever known was when Charles was obliged to be sent to the Hill Provinces for change of air; but this was only for a season.

The family lived in a commodious bungalow in the middle of a large lawn, in which were many gay flowering shrubs; but no pretty flower-beds, as there would be in England, for fear of harbouring snakes; and the walks that led to the garden were of rough gravel on the same account. This garden afforded no amusement to the little boys; for all the time which could be passed out of doors was required for exercise—there was none that could be devoted to the pleasure of gardening: but to make up for this they had their ponies. Every morning before sunrise Alfred and Charles rode out, and remained as long as the heat was not oppressive. Then they came home and had a refreshing bath, and amused themselves in a shady veranda, feeding their tame animals or birds till breakfast. During the greater part of the year the house was shut up, to exclude the heat till sunset, when, after another bath, the ponies were again in requisition, and the ride continued till bed-time.

It was in the cold season, when the tiresome confinement to the house was not quite so great, that Alfred, after one of his pleasant morning rides, ran into his mother's room whilst she was dressing, exclaiming, "Oh, mamma, I am so glad! I have such good news! Bikoo is come back. You see, mamma, he said he would only stay three weeks, and he has kept his word. He has been away three weeks exactly, not one day longer; and he has walked all the way from Patnah in three days

—only three days walking fifty coss! Could you believe, mamma, that any one could walk a hundred miles in three days? I am sure I could not walk so far in thirty days instead of three; and he made so much haste, that he might keep his word. Was it not very good of him?"

"Yes; it was very good of him to keep his word, and I hope you will always imitate him in this good quality: this is something in which you can imitate him. I fear you must wait some years before you can do so in his walking qualities. When did he arrive?"

"This morning; just now. Chamoo and I passed him as I was trotting home on my pony. He seemed very tired—so tired! And I wanted him to get up behind me; but he would not, and told me to make haste, for the sun was getting hot, and so I did. Bikoo told me his father is not dead, but much better. He stayed with him as long as he possibly could, and then he left all his money with him; and Chamoo told me all the bearers had sent all their money to their families at Patnah by Bikoo. You see, mamma, what a very good man he must be, for they sent all their money by him, because they trusted him."

Alfred's mother smiled, and said "she believed Bikoo had a great many good qualities, and that Alfred was quite right to be fond of this bearer, who had taken great care of him ever since he was a little baby."

"Mamma, are you not nearly ready for breakfast? I see them bringing it from the cookroom; and I hear papa come in; and I am going to tell him my good news! I am sure he will be glad to hear it."

"Yes, I am ready now. So run away and tell your good news."

Alfred's father almost satisfied him with the pleasure he expressed at his good news, and in return, he had something pleasant to tell him; for as soon as they were seated, he said, "I just now met Mr Hall, who says there is to be a *mehla* to-morrow, about four coss off, and he proposes sending his tent and passing the day there, and he wishes us to go too."

"What is a mehla?" said Alfred. "Shall you go?"

"I can answer your first question at once. A mehla is a fair or market, where all sorts of merchandise is brought to be bought and sold. I fear there will not be much in our way to buy, and we have nothing to sell; but the weather is so very pleasant, I think we should enjoy the variety, if you can persuade your mother to answer your second question in the affirmative."

"Oh, mamma, pray say Yes. I should like to go so very much. You know I never was in a tent. Have you any objection, mamma?"

"I should like to go very much too, Alfred. It will be as great a novelty for me as for you; and I have only one objection—How are we to get there, for you have forgotten that the horse is lame?"

"Oh, papa, what are we to do? You forget the gig horse is lame."

"No, Alfred, I did not. Mr Hall will drive me over, and your mother will, I have no doubt, make room for you in her tanjahn."

"That will do very nicely. I am so glad; and Bikoo can go too. Shall we stay all day, papa? Shall we go before breakfast, and stay till night?"

"Yes, we must of course go before breakfast; but we intend returning to dinner. I told Mr Hall, if he sent the tent, we would arrange all other matters. So as soon as old Buxsoo comes from the bazaar, we must give him notice, for it will be quite an undertaking for him, and we must give him time to make due preparations."

Buxsoo the khansaman, an old man with a long white beard, of which he was very proud, soon made his appearance. He had a large white turban on his head, made of many yards of muslin very tightly and neatly folded; and as it was now the month of December, and the weather cold, instead of his fine white cotton dress, he wore a long one made of dark-blue cloth, which was open at the breast, to display a scarlet waistcoat beneath. The upper dress had two rows of very smart buttons down the front, as far as the waist; and round his waist was a sash of red muslin, folded several times about his body; his trousers were large and loose; his shoes of light yellow, turned down at the heels, and with curled pointed toes. But the description of Buxsoo's dress is not yet complete, for he was a person of consequence, and we must not forget to say that his watch-ribbon appeared from a pocket just above his cumberbund or sash. As he came into the house, he left his shoes at the door—for it is not considered respectful to wear them in the house in India, and the natives take them off, as Europeans take off their hats.

When Buxsoo heard of the proposed expedition, he said he would take care that everything should be ready; that he had marched as far as Delhi, and knew how to make all necessary arrangements; and as his mistress had never travelled in this way before, he was quite pleased to show his importance. He found some difficulty in answering all Alfred's questions, who could not contain his joy at the thought of spending a day in a tent. He ran in and out of the room with messages of various kinds from the servants in the veranda, who were all busy talking together of what should be done and what should not.

At first, the bearers thought they could carry the tanjahn without hiring more men; then they commissioned Alfred to tell his mother that they would require four more; then Buxsoo wished to know if he might have one of the mallee's coolies to carry the plates and dishes, or if he should hire one?

"I think the *mallee* [gardener] can spare us a coolie for one day from the garden," said his mother; "and we can take some of the light things in the tanjahn with us."

"Will the coolie carry all the plates and dishes on his head, mamma?"

"No; Buxsoo will pack them carefully in two baskets, with strings attached to them, and these will be fastened to each end of a bamboo, which the coolie will carry over his shoulder, sometimes on one, sometimes on the other, and he will be able to carry a much heavier weight than he could on his head. But look, Alfred, who comes here?"

It was Bikoo, who now came in to pay his respects to his master and mistress, or, as it is called in India, to make his salaam. He had bathed and eaten, and did not look so tired as when Alfred saw him in the morning; and he assured Alfred he should be quite rested and ready to go with him to the mehla the next day.

The next morning Alfred was awake long before daylight; and he thought seven o'clock would never come. It came at last, and he was in the tanjahn the moment it was brought to the door. The morning was cold, and he and his mother were glad to wrap themselves up in cloaks and shawls; and Bikoo and the four house-bearers had on warm jackets made of English chintz, thickly quilted with cotton, which looked very comfortable. The hired bearers wrapped their cotton sheets about them as well as they could, for they had no jackets of any kind, and they looked cold and shivering, till near eight o'clock, when the sun became so powerful, that the head of the tanjahn was obliged to be put up to screen Alfred and his mother from the sun, and then the poor bearers seemed to enjoy its beams. Four of them were required to carry the tanjahn at once, and when they were tired, they changed burdens with the others, who carried a kettle, a small brazier to hold charcoal to boil the water for the tea, and to cook the rice and the fish for breakfast. They also carried two earthen vessels of clean water to drink.

Bikoo did not assist in carrying; he ran by the side of the tanjahn, and pointed out to Alfred everything which he thought his young master would like to notice.

After they had gone about six miles, they came to a small river where an old man and a boy were fishing for mullet, which they caught with a sort of spear like the pictures of Neptune's trident. Bikoo went to the old man and asked him if he would sell some of his fish; but he said he had none to sell, for he was Mr Hall's fisherman, and he had orders to take the fish to his tent at the mehla, instead of to his house as usual; so Bikoo told him he must make haste, or he would be too late for breakfast.

The road was now thronged with people going to the mehla: some men on ponies, but many more walking—all of them muffled up, to keep them from the cold morning air: the better-dressed had muslin turbans on their heads, and thickly-wadded jackets, or long cloth caftans, or coats, with a shawl worn like a plaid; and as they were on horseback, shoes turned down at the heel, and pointed at the toes, and of various colours. The travellers on foot were not so gaily dressed; most of them were nearly covered by large coarse chintz quilts instead of shawls; and their thick strong black shoes, not turned down at the heels, showed they were intended for use, not show. The women had their faces painted with various streaks of different colours, and a pretty sparkling sort of wafer stuck on their foreheads. Their earrings were very large, but they were not all *rings;* some of them had leaden cylinders stuck in the lobe of their ears, and their arms were covered with bracelets made of a white metal; their only dress was a long sheet twisted several times round the body, and one end brought over the head like a veil: most of them had a little child sitting astride on one hip, and a basket or metal pot on their heads. Then there were carts with their creaking wheels and small half-starved oxen. Then they passed one or two larger carts with dome-like tops and white curtains, closely shut, to conceal the females of higher rank, who would on no account allow themselves to be seen; and so, poor ladies, they could see nothing. These carts were drawn by very large and handsome white oxen, with their horns painted red, and bells about their necks, and with their gay trappings, looked very stately. In all the crowds they passed, and all they overtook, they saw no one like themselves—not another European.

The hum of many voices now made our party aware that they were close to the mehla; and immediately they were at the tent which they were to occupy. It was pleasantly pitched under a mangoe tree; and goats, for the sake of their milk, were in attendance.

Alfred was out of the tanjahn and into the

tent in an instant. The table was laid for breakfast as comfortably, and with as much care, as if it had been in a room; and indeed the inside of the tent looked like a small neat room, with a gaudy large pattern paper on its walls, and a roof which rose to a point in the centre. This roof was supported by a strong pole, painted yellow, firmly fixed into the ground: the sides of the tent were about six feet high, and so firmly fastened to the ground, that no one could have imagined they were only canvas lined with gay chintz; there were three chairs, and a bright cotton carpet on the ground. Alfred was delighted.

"Who could have fancied, mamma, when the cart went away yesterday evening with those large bundles piled up on it, that they would have turned into this pretty room, with a passage all round it, and two doors? Do come and look out on this side! The old fisherman has brought the fish, and the kitmutgars are cooking them, and the bearers are boiling the water; and then come and look out at the other door, we can see the mehla. Look, mamma, do you see those men going along? Are they snake men do you think? They have not got yellow dresses, and their baskets are not like snake baskets."

"No, they are not snake men, though I have no doubt there are plenty of them at the mehla. But these men are carrying Ganges water to sell."

"Do you mean water from the river Ganges? What have they got it in? And what are they going to sell it for?"

"They have got it in small bottles, and they will find many purchasers for the waters of the holy river, as the natives consider the Ganges. They believe it to be a charm, and to give holiness to those who are sprinkled with it, and that a promise made in presence of this water is more binding than without it. It is sold all over India; and devotees from the farthest parts of the country make pilgrimages to bathe in the river, and bring away a little of the water. The greatest mehla in India is held at Hurdwar, at the source of the Ganges; half a million of people frequent it in ordinary years, but every twelfth year the number is increased to at least a million, and the fair is then called a *coom*. Horses, shawls, tents, carpets, jewels, in fact all kinds of merchandise, are sold there; and the natives go to bathe in the holy stream. The same thing takes place on the Nerbudda, and other holy rivers. The ceremonies of bathing and praying last five days; and I have heard many people say it is worth a long journey to see the curious assemblage. In passing down the Ganges, you may see half-a-dozen of these fairs in a single day, each with a concourse of people equal to the population of a large city. At night, the tents and booths are illuminated, and the scene is very striking; but perhaps the most curious thing to an Englishman is the total absence of riot or disorder among such a crowd. European gentlemen go to shoot in the neighbouring jungle, leaving their little boys and their mammas in the midst of the fair without the least apprehension. But if you do not make haste and come to breakfast, we shall not be able to see what is to be seen after our short journey."

Breakfast was soon over, and Alfred told his father that Bikoo was ready with the great red chattah; so they set off together towards the crowd. As they drew near, the hum hum, as Alfred called it, was changed into screaming, chattering, scolding, till at last he said, "Papa, do you think we had better go on ?—What are the people so angry about ?"

"They are not angry at all; they always make this noise when they are buying and selling. The sellers and buyers are both eager to make good bargains; they think of nothing but getting as much money as possible for their merchandise; for you know they always ask much more than they intend to take. Loud voices, however, you must have observed, are universal among the peasantry. The reason perhaps is, that they live almost wholly in the open air, where one requires to speak out more than in a room. Let us go and see what they have got."

"I don't see anything, papa," said Alfred rather disconcerted, "that we can buy."

"No; they did not think of what we should want I daresay, but of what would be required by all this crowd of customers. Look, there are heaps of various kinds of grain, and mustard-seed, and linseed to make oil; and there are the beans to make castor-oil, and sugar: and observe also what a great number of jars. These contain clarified butter, or *ghee:* you have seen the ghee which the bearers use for their cooking instead of butter, and which is sometimes burned in the lamps?"

"Yes, papa, I have seen it often; and owing, I suppose, to the butter being melted, it will keep *good* a long time; so that it does not require to be made fresh every morning, as our butter is. Look, papa, there are plenty of very nice cocoa-nut pipes, and brass water-pots and dishes, but we do not want any of these."

They walked on: now they came to a cloth merchant with bales of cotton cloth, some white, some coarse chintz; then to a stall where shoes of all kinds and colours were displayed, red, green, yellow, turned down at the heels, and with the long-peaked toes turned up, and some of them embroidered on the front with silver; then there were strong shoes for walking with the toes not so pointed, and the heels not turned down. Another merchant displayed small skull-caps, most of them white, but some of various colours, and a few trimmed with narrow gold and silver lace; strings of beads, bracelets of various metals, ornaments for the ears, necklaces made of the shells called cowries, small looking-glasses, coarse combs, and fans or punkahs made from the leaves of the palm-tree.

Then on the next stall were coarse wooden toys —cups, jars, barrels—coloured red, and yellow, and brown.

Alfred and his father now went to look at a small tent beyond a cluster of bamboos: it was just like a gipsy's tent in England. Alfred found his mother and Mr Hall already there, looking at two beautiful Nepal dogs, quite as large as those that come from Newfoundland, but not so gentle; and Mr Hall said that they were not to be trusted, so they could not be bought.

They were going away from the tent, when one of the men brought from under the tent some very fine tails of the Yah or Thibet cow.

"Papa, here is something at last that you can buy; what beautiful long thick white tails! Your syce told mamma a few days ago that the *chowries* * were of no use, and he could not help the flies teasing the horses, for the chowries would not drive them off; now these immense tails will make three or four chowries I am sure."

Alfred's father agreed with him, and two very

---

* A chowrie is a whisk for driving away flies.

fine cow-tails were bought and taken to the tent in the mangoe grove, whither they were all very glad to go, and get under the shade of the thick and lofty trees. There the servants were all busily engaged in cooking and eating their morning meal. The horses were fastened in a sheltered spot, the lazy languid goats were lying down with their eyes shut, as if they were asleep; whilst above them the trees seemed almost alive with squirrels springing and jumping from branch to branch.

Little Alfred was very happy; he ran round and round the tent, jumping upon the pins to which the ropes were fastened that kept the tent secure, running in to beg his father and mother to come out and look at some new sight every five minutes, which, though new to him, was not equally so to them, and it required some persuasion to induce them to lay down their books and come and look at some people they had never seen before, at least that he had never seen before. Bikoo told him they were *Nutts*, and they could do very wonderful things, if his papa would allow them.

His father told him they were Nutts, or gipsies, and that they were in the habit of travelling from one end of India to the other, and that he might desire Bikoo to tell them to exhibit some of their tricks. Upon obtaining this permission, a very old man, almost bent double, immediately squatted himself down on the ground, and began beating his drum with all his might, and screaming out that they should soon see most wonderful things. To perform the wonderful things, a very strong young man and a boy were fixing a bamboo about thirty feet high firmly in the ground; whilst they were doing this, another man began running round and round singing in a monotonous tone.

"Is that all, mamma?" said Alfred. "Anybody could do that."

"Stop, do not be impatient; look!" And Alfred found, whilst he had turned back his head to his mother, that a woman had jumped on the shoulder of the man; yet he was running round and round quicker than before.

"Oh, mamma, this is something!"

And now, when Alfred looked again, the woman stood on the man's head! On ran the man, but the woman stood quite steady; the old man beat the drum louder and louder, and screamed more shrilly than ever; and then the boy went up with an earthen pot in his hand to the man who was running; and before Alfred knew what was coming next, the earthen pot was on the man's head, and the woman on it, and round and round the man ran still!

When this daring feat was performed, the strong man who had been fixing the pole into the ground came forward, and took a large stone ball, and played with it as if it had been a small leathern one with surprising dexterity, catching it first on one shoulder, then on the other, on his arms and feet, as well as his hands. Then he played with two ivory balls at once, then three, then four, till at length eight balls were all in motion at the same time, and it seemed impossible that one pair of hands could propel them all. After he had concluded, the others were rested, and began again. They had prepared a large, flat, circular brass dish, in which they had placed four little wooden pillars about three inches high; on these four flat sticks were laid, and then four more pillars, then four sticks again, till they were thirty-two in all, and on the top of these was another brass dish. The man commenced running in his circle, and by degrees the brass dishes and wooden pyramid were on his head, and the woman on the top of all! To the amazement of everybody, she was as steady as if she had been running round on the ground; and the pyramid was so accurately built, that not one pillar moved out of its place!

Alfred was so much astonished, that he could not speak, could not even be afraid, till at last he was roused by the natives around clapping their hands, and crying "Wah—wah!" After this the two men and the boy climbed up the bamboo very nimbly; but no one thought much of their performances in comparison with those of the woman, who rested for a few minutes, and then began to exhibit again. Before they knew what to expect, she was seen standing on the shoulders of the young man, and he was mounted on the shoulders of the other, and then she was at the top of the tall bamboo. For a moment she leant on it as if to rest; and then extending her arms and legs, lay flat on the very point of it. One of the men followed her, and touched her foot, and then she spun round and round like a weathercock.

"Papa, how *can* she do that?" cried Alfred, scarcely believing what he saw. "Did you ever see anything so wonderful? But I am afraid she will hurt herself very much."

"It is very clever, but she does not hurt herself; she has a belt fixed round her waist, with a sort of iron thimble in front, which fits the iron point at the end of the bamboo. Still, it is astonishing agility."

"How could she learn such wonderful things, papa?"

"By beginning when she was very young, and practising day after day. She could not have learned to do all this when she was grown up. Almost everything can be learned best in childhood; therefore, my boy, make good use of yours, and do not let it slip away unemployed. Here are some rupees which you may give to the people, and let them go, for our tiffin is ready."

After tiffin was over, and the servants had visited the mehla once more, they began to make preparations for returning home. All the plates and dishes were packed up and put carefully into the baskets, and given to the coolie. The shepherd drove his goats homeward, the horse was put to the *buggy*, or gig, and the bearers brought the tanjahn. Mr Hall and

Alfred's father wished to see the ruins of a fine mosque which was at no great distance, and it was settled they should go to it, and then overtake the tanjahn. Whilst they were taking their seats in it, Alfred saw the *calassies*, or tent-pitchers, beginning to take down the tent to pack it on the cart, whilst the heavy oxen were quietly grazing till it was loaded. There was nothing else to be seen of all that had been there in the morning.

"I am very sorry, mamma, that this day is over," said he. "At first I did not care for the mehla, the people made so much noise, and there was such a bustle and confusion; but I am so glad I saw the Nutts—I never saw anything so wonderful; and I am so glad Bikoo came back, that he might see them too."

"And the next pleasure will be to get home and have your supper, and creep into your own little bed, for you look quite tired and sleepy already."

"Oh no, mamma, I am not in the least sleepy, though it is nearly dark, and there is the *masalchie* * lighting his lantern, and there are one

---

* An assistant to the cook and kitmutgars.

or two stars shining out. I wish, mamma, we had twilight in India as you say there is in England; for if there had been twilight, we should have got home before dark. But we are not very far off now, mamma; here are the large tamarind-trees. What a strange thing it is, the bearers will never sit down under them, they are such beautiful trees!"

"Their caste think some evil will happen to them if they rest under their shade."

"But you do not think so, mamma?"

"No, my dear. Your father and I often rest under them when we are riding out in the morning, to show them we have no such fears."

"Look, mamma! What is that on the road-side—that dark log?"

"I do not know, my dear, but we will stop and inquire."

"It is a man, mamma—I am sure it is a man."

And when the bearers stopped, which they were not willing to do, it was found that Alfred was right: it was a man so sick and weak, that he could neither speak nor move. Alfred's mother got out of the tanjahn, and he followed her, and his bearer was by his side.

"Oh, mamma, do you think he is dead?"

"No, my dear, he is not dead; I hear him breathing. He seems faint for want of food."

Alfred looked up at his bearer and said, "Perhaps if you would give him a little water, Bikoo, it would do him good."

But Bikoo shook his head, and said, "No; the man was only a coolie; and a bearer could not help him—he was not of their caste."

Alfred's mother knew what Bikoo said was the case, and that she could not prevail on them to assist the poor dying man, or make them understand how cruel they were. So she said she would wait where she was till Alfred's father came, and then they would see what was to be done. Alfred listened anxiously for the sound of the wheels and the cries of the syces running before to warn passengers to get out of the way of the carriage. In about a quarter of an hour he heard them coming, and cried, "Take care, papa, you do not run over us here. We are waiting for you: we want you and Mr Hall very much: we want you to take a poor sick man to the hospital." Alfred's father and Mr Hall jumped down, when they found what was the matter, and lifted up the poor man into the gig, and then drove off, whilst Alfred and his mother followed as fast as possible.

"How lucky it was, mamma, we saw the poor man! If we had not found him, I daresay he would have died. It is quite dark now; and hush! do you hear the jackals, mamma? They would have attacked the poor man, and he could not have driven them off. How dreadful it would have been! I do not like to think about it. I am so sorry Bikoo would not help him; he is such a good man, and he went all the way to Patnah to see his sick father, and yet he would not give even a little water to this poor man. Oh, mamma, I am so sorry!"

"I am very sorry too, my dear boy—very sorry that poor Bikoo does not know the parable of the good Samaritan; does not believe in Him who told us that parable; does not know that even a cup of cold water given to those who need it is given to Him; does not know that all are equal in His sight. My dear child, you are quite right to be sorry for poor Bikoo; and let us hope that he and all his countrymen will soon learn the pleasure of assisting even the very lowest coolie, and of showing as much love and kindness to them as to the holiest Brahmin. But here we are at home, and here is your father coming from the hospital with news of the poor man."

Alfred was rejoiced to find that the poor man was much revived, and only wanted some food and a few hours' sleep. He was so tired himself, he could scarcely keep his eyes open whilst he ate his supper, and was asleep before the mosquito curtains were tucked safely round his bed.

THE INDIGO FACTORY.

And now the rainy season was at its height; and what was little Alfred doing? He was no longer the same joyous merry boy who had enjoyed his visit to the mehla, and passed the day in the tent under the mangoe tope. No; all around his father's bungalow was either under water, or covered with grass as tall as himself; and he was very ill with fever, unable to raise his languid head from his hot pillow. His father and mother watched anxiously beside his bed; and Bikoo never quitted him, except for a few minutes, morning and evening, to eat the food some of his brother bearers had prepared. He waved the hand-punkah gently over Alfred's feverish limbs, assisted his mother to lift him tenderly when he wished to be moved, and never seemed to require rest himself. At length they had the happiness of seeing a change for the better in the sick child, and soon after, the doctor advised his being taken from the station, for change of air; and as a friend of theirs, who had an indigo factory about fifty miles off, had often begged them to pay him a visit, they took this opportunity of doing so.

The rainy season begins towards the end of June, after the extreme heat, and by the end of July, all the rivers have overflowed their banks, and many wide plains are under water. No one in England can understand the grateful feeling of the first heavy fall of rain, after all around has been parched and thirsty for weeks, and the trees looking as bare, and leafless, and withered as during an intense frost in Northern Europe; then they burst into leaf as if by magic, and in one night the grass seems to spring up, and a carpet of verdure to replace the sandy desert.

But by the end of July the dry season is sometimes regretted, and particularly by travellers who have a land journey to make; and so it was by Alfred's father and mother.

If it had been the dry cold months, after the rains have ceased in October, or even during the hot months before they have begun, they could have had tents, and travelled as they did when they went to the mehla, early in the morning and late in the evening, and rested during the day under the shade of a mangoe tope. But that was impossible now; so they went dâk, as it is called. Alfred went in the same palanquin with his mother, for he was too weak to be in one alone; his father was in another: and instead of changing horses every eight miles, as the stage-coaches do in England, they changed bearers. There were eight men to each palanquin—four carrying, and four resting. They had four *banghy wallas*, or carriers, with their bamboos over their shoulders, carrying the luggage, which was packed in wicker-baskets covered with leather. These men ran on before the palanquins, at the same pace as the bearers, and uttering the same groaning sound at every step, as if they were tired, or their burdens too heavy.

But this is not the case, for they do it to keep time. And where was Bikoo? He wished to run by the side of Alfred's palanquin, assuring him he could do it without being tired; but though Alfred did not like to be without his bearer, he begged he might be sent on the day before with the other servants that they would require during their visit to Mr Ray. Old Buxsoo did not go, but only two kitmutgars, two bearers, and the ayah. The kitmutgars and the bearers walked, and the ayah had a small cart with one horse. This kind of light cart is called an *ecca*.

As soon after daybreak as possible, the travellers started, to enable them to reach a small indigo factory about twenty-five miles off, where they were to rest during the heat of the day. This was not the direct road, but Alfred could not have travelled without rest, and there was no spot sufficiently dry to pitch a tent; so their best plan was to go round a little. And very glad was poor Alfred when the palanquin was set down in the veranda of the small bungalow, and a kind voice inquired, in Hindoostanee, how the little invalid was. The speaker lifted him out of the palanquin, and carried him into the room where breakfast was prepared, and laid him on a couch under the punkah. This was the manager of the indigo factory, and he was very desirous to get some refreshment for the little traveller. He said his goats were very fine indeed; and so they looked, with their bright sleek skins and long silky ears, when they came to be milked in the veranda. He regretted he had no bread, but Alfred's mother had brought some with her; and there was excellent fish, and eggs, and rice on the table for breakfast, of which the gentleman begged Alfred's father and mother to partake, which they did most willingly; and conversed with him about his factory, for he told them he had been so long there, he knew nothing about the rest of the world, and that he even found it troublesome to speak anything but Hindoostanee.

Alfred's mother asked him if he never saw Mr Ray, to whom the factory belonged. He said he did occasionally, on business; but as he was out of the regular line of road, months often elapsed without his seeing any other European. And she asked him how long it was since he left England.

"It is forty years," said he, "since I left home, and I have been in almost every part of India. For fifteen years, none of the letters I have written to my native place have been answered, and I suppose I have not a relation in the world. I have been in this jungle five years; and except Mr Ray, I see no one. He frequently sends me bread, and sometimes English newspapers. But though this place is retired, it is not so much so as my last situation. And now I can scarcely understand what the newspapers are about, so many changes have taken place in Europe since I was in the habit of hearing about it."

Little Alfred whispered to his mother, who was sitting beside him fanning away the flies with her feather punkah, "Mamma, it is as bad as Robinson Crusoe's island."

After this, Alfred slept for an hour or two, and then they set off again on their journey. But before they went, the kind old gentleman brought some very large sweet limes from his garden for Alfred, who thanked him very much, and felt quite sorry to leave him in his solitary, desolate abode. They had several rivers to cross, but they found boats large enough to hold the palanquins and bearers at the ferries across them. In many places, however, where streams had been formed by the rains, and even deep streams, there were no boats to be had, and the bearers were obliged to put the palanquins on their heads, and so wade across. This was not at all pleasant. However, they met with no accident; and soon after sunset, Alfred revived, and said he felt much stronger, and was amused by looking out at the myriads of brilliant fire-flies on the graceful bamboos. And he watched the men who ran before the palanquins with torches, which they kept alight by pouring oil on them every five minutes from a sort of flask.

"I never saw the fire-flies so bright and beautiful, mamma, and so many of them. I feel so much better now; all day long I have been asleep I think; ever since we left the indigo factory I have seen nothing. Have you been asleep, mamma?"

"No, my dear."

"Then I am sure you must be much fatigued, for you have no room, and your arm must be tired with my head. Will you let me go into papa's palanquin, and then you will be able to sleep?"

"I am tired, my dear little boy, and very glad to find that your own weakness has not made you selfish and unmindful of others. Your father will be very happy to hear your voice, if you are strong enough to call to him: his palanquin is quite at hand."

Alfred was soon nestled comfortably beside his father, who talked to him, and told him stories, and amused him during the rest of the tedious way. At last the bearers seemed to trot along more briskly, and groan louder and louder; and before Alfred knew what they were about, the palanquin was put down in the fine veranda of Mr Ray's handsome house, and Bikoo was waiting anxiously for his little master. He lifted him out immediately, and carried him into a large elegant room, and laid him down on a couch.

Mr Ray welcomed them most kindly; and Alfred liked to look at his good-tempered, happy face, though he was too weak and tired to talk and laugh, as Mr Ray wished him to do; and he was glad to be laid in his comfortable bed as soon as possible, where, before many minutes had elapsed, he fell into a sound sleep, from which he did not awake till the crows and rooks gave notice that day was about to break.

Alfred was not able to go out to ride or walk; but he sat in the west veranda, talking to Bikoo of the adventures of the day before, and telling him of the poor solitary old gentleman in his little bungalow—very different from the beautiful, large, airy house in which they now were. The veranda was a lofty colonnade, and between each pillar green wooden screens descended to within a few feet of the ground, to exclude the glare and sun; but they could not exclude the *flies*, which surpassed anything that Alfred had ever seen in his life before. He observed that, as soon as the servants had prepared the table for breakfast, they put a muslin cover over it, large enough to enclose the cups, saucers, plates, everything that was on it, and in a few minutes this clean white muslin screen was blackened with flies.

"How very disagreeable!" said Alfred to his father, who now joined him. "What can be the reason that there are so many flies?"

"The indigo is the reason," replied his father.

"What is indigo? I have so often intended

to ask you; but I suppose my illness had made me stupid, papa."

"Did you not observe, as we came along yesterday, people cutting a bright green plant, and loading carts with it?"

"Oh no, I saw nothing yesterday till the evening. I am sorry I did not see the indigo; perhaps there will be some when we go back?"

"Not much in the fields, but we shall see it here manufactured and made fit for use. You cannot go through the works to-day, nor perhaps to-morrow, but before we return we shall see it all. Here is Mr Ray coming to breakfast; he has been very busy all this morning."

Mr Ray came in: he had on a very large hat, covered with white cloth; the brim was nearly as large as an umbrella, still his face was quite red and sunburnt, and he looked very different to the gentlemen Alfred had been accustomed to see. He told him that he had been out on his elephant for many hours visiting his fields; that he wished to get his indigo cut and brought in as soon as possible, for if the rivers rose much higher, a great deal of plant would be injured, and what was cut already would be washed away. "And now bring breakfast—bring breakfast quickly, for I hope you are all as hungry as I am," cried he. The servants came in with the breakfast, consisting of fish and rice dressed in various ways, several kinds of new-baked bread, fresh-made butter, eggs and omelets, and fruit. Before taking off the muslin cover to put them on the table, the bearer began pulling the large heavy punkah, which had also a deep fringe at the bottom of it; this dispersed the flies; and the moment the dishes were on the table, each kitmutgar began to whisk about his chowrie vigorously, to keep them away; and the tea was scarcely poured into the cups, before a silver cover was put on, to keep them out of it. These precautions are always more or less necessary during the rains in India; but Alfred had never seen such swarms of these troublesome insects before, and had never understood what a plague they must have been in Egypt.

"I am very busy just now," said Mr Ray as soon as breakfast was over. "I must go to the works immediately." He asked Alfred's father to go with him; and if he was not afraid of the heat, to take Alfred to see the indigo in the vat; saying that they would not have far to go, as unfortunately it was too near the house, which was the reason they were visited by so many flies. Alfred said he should like to go, and Bikoo carried him in his arms, and another bearer carried a large umbrella over his head, and they went with Mr Ray. Alfred found that what was called a vat, was a building about forty feet long and thirty broad. They went up some steps outside, which led to a platform within the building, from which they looked down upon a sort of immense bath; there was, however, no water in it, but there was a great quantity of the indigo plant. Whilst they were watching, Mr Ray ordered the water from the reservoir to be let on. It poured into the vat; and there, Mr Ray said, it must remain for about fourteen hours untouched; and by the time Alfred was up the following morning, the next process would not be quite completed. Alfred was glad to get into the cool house, and he amused himself with looking at a great many beautiful prints which Mr Ray kindly lent him; and then, when his eyes were tired, which they soon were, he lay down and slept.

In the evening, he went with his mother into

the large garden, in which there were no beds of pretty flowers as in England, and no English vegetables, for these only thrive in the cold season; and instead of peas and lettuces, and cauliflowers and cabbages in June and July, they do not appear in India till December. There were no flower beds, but there were some beautiful creepers and large handsome flowering shrubs. The plums, and peaches, and grapes were all over, but there were oranges and limes on their bright green trees; and the custard-apple, so rough and scaly without, and so sweet and pulpy within; and the luscious guavas, and the refreshing pine-apples; and at the end of the garden was a row of plantain-trees, each with its gigantic blades of leaves, and its immense bunch of fruit. Then there were gourds of all kinds, and cucumbers, and water-melons. But an Indian garden, except during the cold weather, offers few attractions, and Alfred and his mother spent the rest of the evening in the veranda.

The next morning the little boy was able to get up and accompany Mr Ray to the vat. As he went up the steps, he heard strokes, as of so many oars splashing in a river, and men shouting and screaming with all their might, as the natives always do when they wish to exert their strength. When he got to the top of the steps, he saw twelve men standing in a very dark-blue liquid; they had scarcely any covering on their bodies, which were dyed of a very dark blue, and they had long sticks in their hands, with which they struck the dark liquor.

Mr Ray told Alfred that this was called the *beating vat*, and was not the same building he had been in the day before. The plant, he said, had been steeped in that vat fourteen or sixteen hours, and had all become *decomposed* in the water, which was quite green at the end of that time, and was then allowed to run into this vat. Men had been employed beating it, as Alfred saw them doing, for three or four hours; and as the green liquid was now become blue, they were going to leave off.

"Then what will become of it?" said Alfred.

Mr Ray said that the water would then be left until the *sediment* had settled at the bottom; then the water would be allowed to run off, and a most beautiful soft, blue, pulpy matter would be found on the smooth floor of the vat, like very thick cream.

"Then what is done with this?"

"Why, the next thing is to boil this blue cream till no froth or scum rises, and it is as smooth as—what shall I say?—as liquid glass. But come, you look quite tired, and we will finish our talk about indigo after breakfast. Before we have bathed and dressed it will be ready."

Alfred *was* tired, and glad to get away from the disagreeable smell of the indigo and the stupifying noise of the beaters.

After breakfast, Mr Ray gave Alfred a cake of indigo of about three inches. "Now," said he, "we must make the indigo cream you saw this morning into little blue cheeses like this. After the liquor you saw has been boiled, it will run out into huge sieves, made by stretching coarse cloth over frames of wood; the water will run through by degrees, and leave the indigo of much the same consistency as cream cheese. But we must not be satisfied with it in that state, for we have to pack it up and send it to Calcutta, from whence it travels to all parts of the world. Then we must take this soft substance and put it into boxes, of which the bottoms are perforated; and as the indigo is screwed down very tightly by means of machinery, every particle of moisture is squeezed out, and then we cut it into cubes, and put it for three months into the drying-house."

"What a very great deal of trouble is required to make indigo!" said Alfred sighing, as if he were quite tired with merely listening to the process. "And what is the use of it after all? I see it is a beautiful blue paint, but I should think all the painters in the world would not use so much indigo as you can make in this one factory."

Mr Ray laughed heartily as he said, "Our indigo would scarcely be worth making, even for painting, if there was none else to be had; but the great use of indigo is for dyeing. It is required not only in dyeing blue, but is necessary to produce almost every other colour; and you would be quite astonished if you could understand how much indigo is sent away from Bengal every year. This is one of the great businesses which England has given to India instead of the cotton manufacture, destroyed by our machinery; and the facility and intelligence with which the Hindoos have glided into it are quite wonderful. But you are not old enough to care much about these matters yet, and I must be off to my work instead of talking here."

Alfred was very much obliged to Mr Ray for taking so much pains to explain to him all about his business; but he thought he should not like to live always at an indigo factory. The flies and the disagreeable smell distressed him; and the coolies who worked at the factory looked so thin, and their skins were of such a dreadful colour.

Alfred's father could not be absent from his station; so he had left him and his mother with Mr Ray, who was very kind indeed. He played and romped with Alfred, and told him droll stories of what he did when he was a little boy at school, explaining to him all about the amusements and pleasures of English boys, which seemed very strange to Alfred, who was still languid, and easily tired, though he was every day more and more able to enjoy himself.

At the end of a fortnight, his father came to take him and his mother home, to which Mr Ray very unwillingly consented; but as they must go, he proposed that they should make a little round the first day, to visit a friend of his who had a remarkably fine factory, and said that he would go with them so far, and lend his elephant for Alfred and his mother. Alfred was delighted at the thoughts of this; he had never been on an elephant, and he knew this one was very well trained, and particularly gentle.

The next morning, Chunee—that was the name of the elephant—was ready at daybreak to take Alfred from Searle factory. He had been very happy there—every one had been kind to him, and he had got stronger and stronger every day. He was sorry to go, but he had many pleasures in prospect to make him forget his regrets, and the first was his ride on Chunee. She was covered with a handsome scarlet cloth, and on her back was the houdah, or seat, large enough for Alfred and his mother. The moment she was desired, Chunee knelt down, and the steps were put against her side, to enable them to mount up into the houdah. The mahout, or driver, sat with his legs across her neck, as if he had been on the back of a horse; he had neither reins nor whip, but an iron instrument in his hand, with which he struck the top of the animal's head. As soon as she was bid, she rose up gently and walked on very quickly, but still so smoothly, that the motion was agreeable.

"Oh, mamma, this is very pleasant! But I hope the man will not hurt her with that iron thing in his hand?"

"No, my dear; the mahout seems merely to tap her head, and she obeys his voice, and is guided by that more than anything else. Turn round your head, and you will see that there is a man running behind with a goad, but he does not seem to touch her; and indeed she does not require it, she steps out so willingly."

"This is much pleasanter than travelling shut up in a palanquin, for we can see all round us, mamma. There are the coolies taking away the mat doors from their huts, and sitting down on the ground to wash their mouths, and then they will set off to the factory to work. But look, mamma! that is not an indigo field?"

"No, my dear; that is rice, which requires more moisture than any other grain, and will not grow properly unless the roots are under water."

"They would not be very pleasant fields to walk through. Though we are on the back of the elephant, instead of in the palanquin, there is not much to be seen, mamma—all round nothing but fields, and clumps of bamboos, and a few trees. I wish there were some hills; I should like to see some hills, for I can scarcely fancy what a hill is like. I wish you had gone to the hills with Charles, and that we had all gone, instead of letting him go with Aunt Mary."

"I wish we could all have gone too; but that could not be, and he will soon be home again, and you will see him."

"I shall be *very, very* glad indeed to see him; but I should like to see hills too, such hills as you and papa talk about as being in Scotland."

"I hope you will see them some time or other, and get rosy cheeks climbing up their purple sides."

"Look, look, mamma! What beautiful white clouds are rising over that clump of bamboos so very white and pointed!"

"I do not see any clouds, my dear."

"Oh yes, mamma. Now look a little this way over the palm-trees; they are tinged with red; the sun will soon rise from behind them.

But I do not think that is the east, for the sun set there last night. Oh, mamma, you surely see the clouds now?"

"I see what you are pointing to, but they are not clouds. Look again, and try if you cannot discover what they are. You shake your head; you cannot discover: they are the snowy peaks of the Himalaya Mountains, and the rosy tinge upon their summits is caused by the reflection of the sun, not yet risen to us, but shining brightly on them."

"Oh, mamma, how very grand—how very beautiful! I see now they are not clouds; I see their sharp peaks as if they were *cut out*. And now it is lighter, I see hills much lower, and like what I fancied hills to be."

"Yes, there are several lower ranges which, as you say, look like *hills*. But no one can imagine the grandeur and beauty of the snow-clad Himalayas—the loftiest mountains in the world."

"And, mamma, Charles is in the Himalaya? Write to him, and tell him that we have seen the hills where he is. I am so glad I have seen them!"

"I might almost as well write and tell Charlie

that the same sun shines on us by day and the same moon by night; for the Himalayas extend from one end of India to the other, and he is in one of the lower ranges, not amongst these mighty snow-clad peaks."

Alfred continued to gaze with wonder and delight for some time, and then they talked of the Alps, and the Apennines, and the Andes; but he could not help being pleased to find that no mountains in the world were so high as those he had seen—the Himalayas.

Before the sun was oppressive they reached Paget factory. Mr Ray and his father were waiting for them, to help them down from their pleasant seat on gentle Chunee. If Alfred had been left to himself, he would have tumbled down the ladder head foremost, so eager was he to tell of the grandeur of the Himalayas; and even Chunee's merits were for a few minutes forgotten. However, he did not go into the house without patting her rough sides, and thanking her very courteously for the pleasant ride he had had.

There was much to be seen at Paget factory besides making indigo. The gentleman who lived there amused himself with taming all sorts of animals, and allowed them to walk about his pretty house as cats and dogs do in England. There was a young bear rolled up comfortably in one corner of the room; and in another corner a large basket contained two very young leopards, not larger than cats usually are, and not nearly so large as a fine white Persian grimalkin, with its long bushy tail, which was so tame, that it came whenever its master called, and sat upon his shoulder. The veranda was full of monkeys, and a mungoose was playing about.

Alfred thought the mungoose a pretty little animal, but asked what was the use of keeping it: and Mr Ray told him it was of very great use in killing snakes; and as long as one was in the house, there was no danger of being killed by a cobra capella, no fear of finding one coiled up in the wash-hand basin, as he had done a few months ago.

The very mention of a cobra capella made Alfred shudder, he had heard so many stories of it from his bearer. And it is no wonder that men should be afraid of a creature whose bite is fatal in a few hours.

"Did you ever see a cobra capella?" said Alfred.

"Frequently," replied Mr Ray; "and the last one was upwards of four feet long, and four inches in circumference. It had got into one of the rooms of my house by means of a rat's hole, and was seen by the sirdar reposing quietly under the matting of the floor."

"Oh what did you do?"

"Cut him in two with a sword; upon which he emitted a sound which I can only liken to a loud roar, and thrust his black head far beneath the matting to take his revenge. But he was too completely disabled to do mischief, and we soon finished him."

"Yet there are men who take hold of these snakes with their hands?"

"There are indeed. I have heard many persons doubt the reality of the snake-charmers' performances; but I have seen them with my own eyes, and in circumstances where deception was impossible. On one occasion we led the snake-charmers, who had come from Benares, to a distant and uninhabited house, making them leave their baskets of snakes behind them; and on arriving at the spot, obliging them to untwine their waistcloths and turbans, to let us see that they had nothing whatever about them but the hollow gourd on which they played their buzzing music. We now set them to work among the thick grass near a ruined tank; and very soon one of the men darted his hand into a large prickly bush, but drawing it back again, recommenced his tune. A second dash of his hand brought out an enormous snake, which he almost threw into my face! It was a cobra capella; and the snake-charmer made it dance to his music, raising and drooping its head according to the tune. On examining the creature afterwards, we found that both the poison fangs were perfect; and there was no longer any room for doubt."

"How wonderful!" exclaimed Alfred. "But have you no more stories to tell?"

"I have only to say that I saw various other instances of charming, both when the snakes were poisonous and harmless. Sometimes, however, the professors are not so fortunate; for I have lately read in a Calcutta paper of two of them having lost their lives by the bite of a cobra capella which they were exhibiting. I have myself seen eight snakes crawling over a man's body at once, and putting their forked tongues between his lips."

"Dreadful!"

"But doubtless the poison fangs of these reptiles had been previously extracted." Alfred now looked at the mungoose with great respect, but was puzzled to know how such a pretty little creature could combat successfully a cobra capella. Mr Ray replied that it was a mystery to more than him; although the fact was well authenticated, that the mungoose possessed a knowledge of some specific which protected him from the fatal effects of the bite of the snake. In the frequent combats which take place between these natural enemies, the mungoose is always observed to run away among the grass and shrubs when wounded, and he speedily returns in a condition to resume the fight. The conclusion is, that he has eaten something which neutralises the poison; but no one has yet discovered what it is.

Alfred was much amused looking at the monkeys, but he could not be prevailed on to play with the leopards. He could not help wondering how the gentleman had been able to get such very young creatures away from their mother. but he told him that they were found nearly drowned in the river a week before. They had evidently been washed away by the inundations, and he was glad to get them instead of a fine full-grown leopard that he had sent away some months ago.

"But," inquired Alfred, "did you keep a full-grown leopard running about the house?"

"When I was quite alone," said the gentleman, "I did keep it going about, and it never injured any one; but my sister and her children came to see me, and to spend a few months here, and then she begged me to put him in a cage."

"And you did so, did you not?" said Alfred, looking as if he dreaded to hear the contrary.

"Yes, I put him in a cage, but it was not a very strong one. However, the confinement made him ferocious, and one day he really alarmed us all."

"How was it? Pray tell me, sir?"

"Why, there was a tremendous storm: I have been in India a great many years, but I never remember such a violent *toofan* [squall]. My sister was afraid the roof of the bungalow would be blown off, and I had some fears of the same kind; so I took her and the children into my little dressing-room, which was more protected than any other room in the house. We were scarcely in, when we heard the cry that the leopard was loose, and in the middle room. I wanted to go out immediately and secure it; but something had fallen against the door of the dressing-room, and it was impossible to open it. In the meantime none of the servants dared approach the animal, and he kept them all at bay, lashing his tail and showing his teeth; but fortunately, in one of the whisks of his tail, the tip whisked through the Venetian door, and a bearer outside caught hold of it, and held it firmly till some more men came to his assistance, and threw a noose over the vanquished foe. After this I was afraid to keep him, and gave him to the captain of a ship to take home for his education; and perhaps he may now be in the Zoological Gardens in London, where I sent a fine bear, which required more attention to form his mind and manners than I could bestow on him."

Alfred was very glad these animals had been sent away before he came; he was better pleased to hear of them than to see them.

Near the house was a very pretty small lake;

great pains were taken to keep it free of weeds; and on it was a small boat painted green and white. About half an hour before sunset, Alfred and his father and mother got into the boat, and Mr Ray and his friend rowed them about the lake. Alfred was delighted, and very sorry when it was too dark to remain on the water any longer, and tried to persuade his mother he was not in the least tired; however, as soon as he was in the house, he was glad to go to bed.

"To-morrow by this time we shall be at home, mamma; and I shall see my pony, and my parrot, and my goat, and I shall be so happy; but to-day I have been on an elephant, I have seen the Himalaya Mountains, and I have rowed in a boat. I shall never forget this day as long as I live."

THE MORNING RIDE.

I shall tell you no more stories of Alfred whilst he was alone, for I think you must wish to hear of his brother Charles, who returned home very soon after Alfred's pleasant visit to the indigo factory; and after the family had removed to another station situated on the banks of the Ganges, Charles's residence in the hills had made him quite strong and well, and he was able to run about and play with his brother, instead of lying all the morning under the punkah, as he used to do before he went away. He was the best-tempered little fellow you can imagine; he looked rather grave and sedate; but he was really full of fun, though he did not look so lively and quick as Alfred, who always took the lead in all they did. Charles always wished to imitate his brother—to do what he did, and to go where he went. He thought all he said or did must be right; and was satisfied in all their plans for amusement to be guided by him. Alfred, in return, was very kind, and did not take advantage of Charles's readiness to yield to him, but played fairly; and thus they were always happy, and did not dispute nor disagree. They were in the habit of telling all they saw, all they did, and almost all they thought, to their parents; and the morning ride generally furnished a subject for conversation at breakfast.

One morning after their return from their ride, Alfred was impatient to tell how he and his brother had been entertained by seeing some people in a mangoe grove making baskets; and he said he should like to return in the evening to buy some. His mother asked what sort of baskets they were.

"They are round straw baskets, mamma, with covers larger round than this plate, and very strong indeed. They only cost two annas each. Don't you think they are very cheap? We can buy one for you and papa too."

"But after you have bought them, I am afraid they will be of no use," said his father.

"Oh yes, they are very useful; you can put anything in them," said Alfred. "We mean to keep everything in ours quite safely."

"What sort of things? Will your kites, or your bats, or your hoops go into these baskets?"

"No, not these large things; but our balls, and our string, and our tops will go in," said Charles.

"But you keep all these quite safely now in the pretty painted boxes that were sent to you from Bareilly, and what is the use of taking them out of the box to put them into the basket?"

"Then don't you think they would be useful?"

"They might, or they might not; but I cannot buy things not absolutely wanted. I have not money enough."

"We could get eight baskets for one rupee," said Alfred, "and four will be sufficient."

"My dear boy," replied his father, "you must learn to conquer desires of this kind. There may be something you would like to buy to-morrow—what was bought yesterday?"

"Nothing, nothing at all, papa," said Alfred.

"Was it not yesterday that the conjurer came who swallowed the sword?"——

"And played with the eggs instead of balls," interrupted Alfred; "and then put a pea into his mouth, and drew out yards and yards and yards of thread: it was very curious indeed."

"Yes, but it cost some money. Your mother and I had often seen them before, and it was only to amuse you that we allowed them to exhibit."

"Well, that was something yesterday, but there was nothing the day before."

"I think it was the day before you got your

tops, and said the strings of your kites were so old, you wanted new ones?"

"Yes, so it was; but the strings of our kites are only thread. You were not at home, papa, when that rajah came outside the fort with his grand tents, and so many servants, and bullock carriages, and horsemen, and chaprasseys? And then, in the evening, he sat outside his tent, and watched his servants flying kites for his amusement. The kites were little things, just like ours, pink, and green, and red, and all manner of colours; but the strings were proper strings, made of silk, and covered with glass, pounded very fine, and mixed with gum; and when one string was pulled against the other, it cut it, and down fell the kite; and the rajah watched them so eagerly, and when the strings were cut, he cried out, 'Wah! wah! wah!' and seemed so pleased. It was a very strange amusement for a grown-up man, I think; but still it must be difficult to pull one string against the other."

"Well, well, we shall consider about the baskets; but it is wrong to spend money we cannot afford, even on useful things. Did you see nothing but these marvellous baskets?"

"Oh yes; a great many other things. We saw a number of squirrels jumping about from branch to branch among the trees; they seemed almost to fly. I tried to catch one little fellow that came very low, but I could not get him; he was out of sight in a moment. They were so pretty, and seemed so happy: I wish I could jump like them from tree to tree. Besides these, we saw a most wonderful creature. We met two hill-men, and one had got a small branch of a tree in his hand, and there was an animal crawling on it. I never saw such a beast before. It did not jump, or run, but went creeping so cautiously and slowly—slowly. I told them to bring it here for you to see. The body is nearly as long as my arm—from the elbow to the wrist I mean—and nearly as thick. Its back-bone sticks up, and its sides press out, and it has no neck at all, and a very curious-shaped head. It is not hairy; it does not shine like a lizard; but it has a dry sort of skin: and then I don't know what colour to tell you it is. It is all sorts of shades, and has got a very long thin tail, and it winds its tail about the stick; but look, papa, there are the men in the veranda!"

"Ah, this is a chameleon, and a very large

one indeed! It is really a curious creature. Look at the eyes; they project far beyond the rest of the head, and it can turn them whichever way it pleases, behind or before: and what is more wonderful, with one eye it can look one way, and with the other quite in an opposite direction!"

"Oh look, papa; it was green just now, pretty, bright green, but now it is nearly covered with black spots! Look at it; pray do. Now it is green again. What is the reason of that?"

"I cannot tell you, Alfred, what is the reason; but you see it is the case. The chameleon takes different shades, from very light yellow, even to green or black. It was formerly believed that the colour depended on the substance the creature was near; but we see that is not the case. And it was also asserted that chameleons never eat, but live on air. If you watch, you will see that this is a mistake also."

"What is it going to do? How attentively it is looking at something! Oh do look what a long tongue it has darted out; it is as long as its body I think! What did it do then? What did it do so for?"

"To catch a fly that was on the leaf—that is the way it takes its food. Perhaps if we watch we may see it catch another; and if it puts out its tongue, you will see it is broader at the tip, and this tip is covered with a gummy substance, to which the poor fly sticks, so that it cannot escape."

"Now it is walking; do look at its toes how long they are, and how fast it clings to the stick with them! I told you how slowly it walked along, as if it were afraid of falling. Now it is falling, poor creature; catch it, papa —pray do!"

"No, it will not fall. Look how curiously it hangs by one of the hind-legs."

"That is very wonderful indeed. But, papa, pray keep this extraordinary creature, we should like so much to watch it; and never mind the baskets."

"But how shall we keep it?"

"We can put it into that large wicker-cage that was made for my pretty green parrot. Don't you think we could put the chameleon in it—and if it can catch flies so easily, it will not want any other food? Do you think it will?"

"Yes, I think it will require more than an

occasional fly. Some years ago I had several, and mine were very fond of sugar moistened with a little water, on which they throve very well, and we can try the same plan with this one."

"Alfred, come here very quietly, will you?" whispered Charles. "This man has got one of them asleep on a stick in this jar. No, it is not quite like it."

"No," said his father; "not quite. That came from the hills too; but it is not alive. That is honeycomb."

"What! growing on a stick? I thought that bees made honey and honeycomb in a beehive."

"Yes, so they do; but they cannot make hives, so they are contented without a house. They attach themselves to the branch of a tree, and build round and round it, till the comb is about as large as your arm; and then they begin another; and when they are full, the poor people near the hills and jungles cut them off to sell. The cells are much smaller, and the wax thinner, than in England."

"Are the bees the same?"

"No, I never saw bees in India so large as those in England. Some natives consider that honey made by the very smallest kind of bees is not good for eating. In Ceylon it is prized above all others. But we must not keep the poor men waiting. I will buy this honey, and tell them to bring me some more."

"And will you tell them to bring you some more chameleons, mamma?"

"No, one will be quite as much as we can take care of: and though we may take a great deal of trouble to provide it good food, it would find much better for itself in its own jungles."

"The men have gone away, and we have quite forgotten to ask them what they call this animal; for it was not chameleon, I am quite sure, nor anything like it. Shall I call them back?"

"No, Alfred, you need not. I think I know the name. Was it not *barrah-roopah?*"

"Yes, that was the name. What does it mean, papa?"

"It means twelve colours. I did not observe so many shades in those I had. Let me try and remember. There was a bluish-gray, yellow, bright-green, and black; there were no others, and the green was the prettiest shade of all. At times, too, my chameleons were marked with dark spots, and when they were ill, they became of a very dirty yellow-green colour, and their skin scaled off. I sometimes put them on a white cloth, but that made no difference in their appearance. But we must close the doors of the veranda, it is getting very hot."

THE ELEPHANTS.

Alfred could not get the gentle Chunee out of his head, and one day asked his mother many questions respecting the elephant.

"You must know, Alfred," said she, "that every country has its own kind of animals suited for its climate. In England, the horse thrives well, and is universally employed for riding and for drawing carriages. But this fine animal is not so well adapted for India, where there are great jungles to be traversed. In India, therefore, the elephant, which is of a great size and power, is of much service. It is believed that in the ages long past, elephants and creatures of a similar nature were common in Europe and other parts of the globe, where there is now no animal of the kind."

"And why is that, mamma? Where have these animals gone?"

"These huge animals are believed to have disappeared, or died out, in consequence of changes in the climate and the alterations which have taken place on the surface of the country; but you must study Natural History, and inform your mind properly about these things."

"And will a time come," asked Alfred, "when elephants will no more be seen in India?"

"Perhaps; but it is to be hoped that they will exist as long as circumstances make their services important. People who travel about the country require them to carry their tents and their luggage; and they are of great use to an indigo factor going about his lands, for he can see much better what is going on when he is on the back of an elephant than in a palanquin or buggy; and besides, the elephants can wade through the small rivers, where bearers and horses could not go."

"Can you tell me, mamma, what is the use of the elephant's trunk?"

"That, my dear, is a beautiful provision of the Creator. The trunk answers the purpose of a hand; with it the elephant can take hold of anything, however minute, pick up its food from the ground, and tear down the branches of trees."

"Do you remember, mamma, the mahout told us that Chunee helped to unload herself when they were out in tents: that was very clever."

"Yes, Alfred; and I remember hearing of a wild elephant in the Goruckpoor district which kept watch in his jungle for the droves of oxen passing by loaded with grain, and then rushed out, seized the largest he could find, and carried ox, and grain, and all off into his retreat."

"What did he want with the bullock, mamma? He would not eat it as a tiger would?"

"No, he did not want to eat the bullock, he wanted the grain; and he could not, with all his cleverness, unfasten the thongs which bound the burden on the back of the ox, so he carried all off together, instead of unloading him."

"Do you think this is a *true* story, mamma?"

"The gentleman who told me the story, Charles, said it was quite true; and as I have no reason to think he would tell me he had seen what he had not seen, I believe it to be true."

"Then that was a very clever elephant, and a very strong one too. Do you think elephants are more clever than any other animals in the whole world, mamma?"

"I do not know what to say, my dear boy; it would take a long time to think, and much more knowledge than I possess to answer that question properly. But I do not think, from all we know of them, that they have nearly so much sagacity and intelligence as a dog. How perfectly a dog not only learns to obey his master's orders, but how conscious he is when he has offended him by disobedience! How devotedly he is attached, and how long he retains his love!"

"I think horses may be compared with elephants," said Charles; "don't you, mamma?"

"Yes, Charles; and from what I know of both, I should think a horse could be taught better than an elephant. They are both, probably, equally docile and tractable for *useful* purposes; but I cannot fancy a troop of elephants could be taught to *amuse* us by acting, as many troops of horses can. I have seen a horse feign himself dead after the explosion of a pistol, and not merely fall down, but absolutely lie as if without life; but what was more wonderful still, others appeared to sink gradually from exhaustion and fatigue, and after making many vain attempts to rise, at length stretched themselves to die. One elephant or two may be taught to perform some tricks, but I cannot think they can equal horses in this respect. At the same time, we must not speak too decidedly, for the experiment has never been sufficiently tried. I think an elephant *looks* particularly dull, and stupid, and heavy, and that may be one reason why we 'are astonished to find it is not so: astonished, too, that an animal of such power, and in its wild state so savage, can be tamed into such docility. Nothing can be more frightful than a troop of wild elephants in the jungles, because, from their size and strength, it is so difficult to venture near enough to kill them. No one could imagine that the mighty beast which stalks through the forest crushing all obstacles beneath the weight of his huge foot, could become as manageable as gentle Chunee; or could be taught to pick its way through the crowded narrow streets of such a city as Benares, where a tall man could stretch from one house to another, if he stood in the middle and extended his arms; nor could we suppose that the animal which had been accustomed to tear up trees by the roots, can be taught patiently to assist to load itself with their branches, and bear them wherever its guide desires."

"Well, mamma, I do not think we can decide which is the wisest beast; but horses, and dogs, and elephants, are wise because they are taught; while there are some beasts that are wise of themselves."

"What do you mean, my dear Alfred? You look as if you were puzzled."

"I mean, mamma, like the beavers, which know of *themselves* how to build those wonderful houses on the great lakes in North America. No man has taught them."

"But God has. This power is called instinct, and is quite a different property from that which we have been speaking about. Capacity to understand and obey the commands of man may be called intelligence."

"Then, mamma, birds and insects are like the beavers."

"Yes, insects show astonishing skill in constructing their abodes. Compare a white ant with the huge pyramids it and its fellows raise: the white ant no larger than a small dew-drop—the ant-hill five or six feet high. This structure could not be raised unless the ants acted in concert, unless they had some means of communicating with each other. And then it is not only the size of these buildings which is so wonderful, but their strength makes them seem, like the hill-forts of the native chiefs, impregnable; and so they are, till the river overflows in the rainy season, and then the rushing impetuous stream sweeps away the mighty structure and its myriads of inhabitants."

"Yes, mamma, white ants are very curious; but I don't think you are sorry when the river washes them away and their forts too. They are so mischievous, eating up and destroying everything they come near; not like the good little bees, that build such curious cells, and make such good honey besides. Mamma, you know you promised to show us silkworms when you had an opportunity."

"I have not forgotten my promise, Alfred; and when we go to Boghupoor, you shall see the silkworms in all their various stages of eggs, worms, cocoons, and moths. It is indeed very wonderful to see worms producing anything so beautiful as silk, but you will not be interested by any intelligence or sagacity in them. Do you remember that very strange insect, Alfred, which"——

"Oh yes, mamma, I know what you mean—the lion-ant. Papa showed us one throwing up the fine earth till it had made a large hole at least as deep as a large tea-cup; and then the cunning creature remained quite still at the bottom of its trap, and the poor ants, which thought they were going to discover some new country, fell into his dreadful claws, and were crushed to death. Yes, mamma, I remember the lion-ant quite well, and I think he was as dreadful as a real lion or tiger—I mean as dreadful for the ants as a lion or tiger would be to us."

"Don't you think it is very cruel to take out tame good elephants to hunt tigers? I think it is very wrong to let them be torn by those savage beasts," said Charles.

"It would be better, to be sure, if the tigers could be killed without doing any harm to the elephants; but they are seldom much hurt, and it is really useful to kill the tigers, that do so much mischief, and can never be tamed."

"But could they not find some other way of killing them, mamma? Could they not shoot them?"

"They do shoot them, my dear. But how are people to get into the thick jungles to shoot them, except on the backs of elephants? The tigers would very soon tear them off the largest horses, even if a horse could get into the thick prickly rose-bushes much higher than themselves. Sometimes the tigers tear the elephants' trunks, and injure the mahouts who are seated on their necks; but those who are most likely to be hurt are the men who accompany the elephants to beat the bushes, and to drive the tigers out of their hiding-places. Some of these drivers are often severely wounded."

"It must be very dreadful to meet a tiger in the jungles, mamma!"

"Yes indeed, Charlie, it must. I knew a gentleman, one of the very best persons I ever knew, who went to the hills—those very hills the chameleon came from; not *your* hills, Charlie—not the Himalaya, but the Kurruckpoor hills. He did not go to shoot tigers; he went to teach the natives who live there, and to preach the gospel of Jesus Christ. He could only remain there during the cold season; he could not go till December, and came away in March. All the rest of the year the district is so unhealthy, that no one but the native hill-men can live there; every one else takes fever, and a great many die."

"And did he die, mamma?"

"Yes, Charles, he did die. But I will tell you about him some other time—all that he tried to do, and all that he suffered. What I am going to tell you now is a story about a tiger. One day he was walking down a very beautiful but winding path, with thick jungle on each side. This path led into a valley, to which he was going. He had some hill-men with him, and one of them had a gun in his hand. As they were walking down the path, a very young buffalo crossed it rapidly about a hundred yards before them, springing from one jungle into the opposite. The man instantly raised his gun to shoot it, but his master put it down, saying, 'Do not kill it; we do not want it, and it will not hurt us.' Whilst he was speaking, a very large tiger was seen to spring after the poor buffalo, and in another instant they heard its death-scream as the ferocious monster seized it."

"Oh, mamma," said Alfred, looking almost as terrified as if he had actually heard the bones crushing and the tiger growling, "what would have become of them if the man had fired?"

"Some of them would certainly have been torn to pieces by the tiger instead of the buffalo; for they had no means of escape—no swift horse, no well-trained elephant to carry them out of the jungles. As it was, they met with no accident, the tiger did not molest them, and they reached the hut where the good gentleman lived in safety."

"I am so glad, mamma. But I have heard that tigers are fonder of the flesh of men than of buffaloes. Is that true, mamma?"

"I fear it is. Not long ago a tiger destroyed three of the letter-carriers between Calcutta and Jubbulpoor, one after the other, and their horses were found grazing unharmed by the roadside. After this, no one could be found to undertake the service, till the people of the district mustered to the number of three hundred, and succeeded in slaying the monster, but not till they had beat the jungle for three days."

"But do look, mamma! Just as we are talking of elephants, there is one going along, and there is another, and another. What very large elephants! How tall do you think they are?"

"I should think about ten feet high. These are very fine animals; but the largest and finest I ever saw, which was sent with some others as a present to the Begum Somroo, was twelve feet high, and I am sure it was taller than these."

"Oh, mamma, here are some more! Make haste, Charles; here are a great many elephants. Come and look at them. One, two, three, four, five!" But the little boys soon found themselves confused, and could not count them accurately.

"Mamma, all these elephants are stopping on the plain outside the fort. What can they be there for? Will you let us go and see them as soon as we are dressed?"

"Yes, Alfred, if your father will take you; but I should not like you to go without him; for amongst so many, some may be vicious and unmanageable."

Alfred and Charles went with their father to see the elephants. They were anxious to know all about them, where they came from, and where so many were going. They learned that they all came from Chittagong, and that they were going to the upper provinces, to be used for carrying tents and stores for the army. Then they wished to know all their names; but though their father kindly stayed with them on the plain till it was dark, they could neither learn nor remember the names of the fifty elephants.

THE BUDGEROW

Steamboats now navigate the Ganges, and form agreeable means of journeying up or down that mighty river; but at the time to which we refer, the only method of conveyance for English families was by *budgerow*. A budgerow is a large and substantial boat, fitted up for conveying passengers: it is divided into two cabins, with a small veranda, which separates the hinder part of the boat from the deck. The deck is raised, and on it stand the *dandies*, or rowers; the number of oars varying from eight to eighteen; and the vessel is under the command of a *mangie*, or pilot, who steers. The stern is very high out of the water, the outside gaily painted white and green; and altogether a budgerow is a very pretty-looking boat.

In a vessel of this kind, hired for the purpose, the family of whom we have been speaking prepared to descend the Ganges to Calcutta. As the voyage would occupy at least a month, and as there are no means of procuring accommodation by the way, it was necessary to have several attendant boats, including a cook-boat, in which provisions might be prepared. Thus travelling in India is always attended with incumbrances; not the least being the number of servants whom it is necessary to employ.

In the great city of Patnah they did not find much to interest them, or detain them from their voyage. Even when close at hand, it was hardly visible at all; and although some European houses were scattered along the banks, with here and there a pagoda or a mosque, the general appearance was mean and disagreeable. The city within the walls consisted of one wide but irregular street, running east and west, and hundreds of other passages narrow and crooked. All were disgustingly dirty, and the houses mean and slovenly. In the hot season, the air is thick with dust; in the rains, the whole place is a sea of mud. But even the ugliness of Patnah seemed respectable, from the greatness of its scale; and there was no end to the wonder of the children when they found themselves descending the river for nine miles before getting out of the suburbs. It was very amusing, too, to see the thousands of native vessels thronging the river, each different from the others, and all picturesque.

The prospect of seeing Calcutta had been very delightful to Alfred, and it was with joy that he heard the order given for the budgerow to move. "There, mamma," cried he, "is the last dandie climbing up into the boat with the rope that held it to the shore coiled round his arm; and now the men are beginning to row, and now we are off. I thought the time never would come, there was so much to be done—the things to be packed, and the boats to be hired, and the horses to be sent off by land. Are you not very glad, mamma, all the bustle is over, and that here we are quietly in the boat at last?"

"Yes, my dear."

"I like being in a budgerow very much," continued he.

"I have no doubt you do this first half hour, but we shall be here three weeks at least; and how will you like these two small cabins all day long, after the large rooms and verandas you have been accustomed to? And no riding in the morning, and perhaps no walking in the evening?"

"The cabins are not so very small, mamma, and there is a nice little veranda in front. It is not so very small neither, for there is the large water-jar in it, and the ayahs have room to sit there. And then all day long we shall have so much to look at; we can watch the dandies, and look out for the cook-boat, and the furniture-boats, and the dhobies-boat; and there is such a pleasant breeze upon the river. I am sure I shall like it very much. Do not you, Charlie?"

Charles thought it very pleasant, but he could not help wishing he could have brought his favourite goat with him. The Hindoos, among whom he had been brought up, are very fond of pets, such as goats or lambs. Even the sepoys, when on the march, take with them their pet lambs; and these pretty creatures, gaily decorated with ribbons, form a very interesting part of the spectacle.

"Will it take three weeks, papa, to reach Calcutta?"

"Yes, Alfred, I am afraid it will. If we could have delayed our voyage for a month, the small rivers would have had water in them; but in May that is very seldom the case, and the mangie thinks we must go round by the Sunderbunds."

"What do you mean by the Sunderbunds, papa?"

"You know, Charles, '*the* river'—the river Ganges—does not go to Calcutta, but only a branch of it, called the Hoogly; and to get from the great Ganges into the Hoogly, we must go by some of the smaller rivers which communicate with the Hoogly."

"But are these rivers the Sunderbunds, papa?"

"No; these rivers have so little water in them, that our boat would not float; in fact in many places they are quite dry, so we must follow the course of the Ganges. Near its mouth it divides into many channels; and the swampy district of country covered with vast forests through which these run is called the Sunderbunds. This name *Soonder Bun* means beautiful wood; but the scene is as desolate and dreary as can well be imagined—a mere labyrinth of creeks and rivers, with walls of forest towering on all sides. By one of the channels I have mentioned we must go; and we shall have to cross a sort of arm of the sea to get into the river which leads to the Hoogly, on which Calcutta is built."

"I hope we shall go that way," said Alfred; "we shall see so many wild beasts, perhaps tigers, and rhinoceroses, and wild buffaloes, and wild hogs. And Bikoo told me he came by the Sunderbunds once, and they heard the tigers quite plainly; and he said one jumped from the shore on the top of the budgerow. But do you believe this, papa?"

"Yes, I *know* it is true."

"That was dreadful!" said Alfred. "I would rather not go by the Sunderbunds. But see what long oars the men have got! It must be very hard work rowing. What is the man doing with that long bamboo in his hand standing up in front of the boat?"

"He is measuring how deep the water is; and when he finds we are near a sandbank, he makes a sign to the mangie, who is at the back of the boat, to steer another way. But he has not been quick enough this time, for here we are on one, and stuck quite fast."

In a moment up jumped all the dandies, threw down their oars on the deck, and sprang into the river.

"Oh do look at the poor men pushing with their backs against the boat, and screaming out so loud! I am afraid they will never be able to move the boat. Oh yes, we are off again, and I hope the man with the stick will be more careful another time."

"The man with the stick, as you call him, Alfred, may be very careful, and yet, as the river is so shallow, we may stick fast very often, for the sandbanks constantly change their places; and even the mighty Ganges is very shallow in many places at this season of the year. But, Alfred, your pleasant breeze is pleasant no longer; it is getting quite hot, and the glare is so great, that we must shut the Venetians."

"Now, papa, how comfortable it is! We move along so smoothly, that you can write at your table, and mamma can read and work, and we can sit down and amuse ourselves in this snug corner. A budgerow is very pleasant."

The first day the voyage was indeed pleasant; they met with no more sandbanks; although now and then the travellers were horrified by seeing a dead body, charred and blackened, float past them on the river. It is the custom of the Hindoos to burn their dead; and when they are too poor to provide themselves with the requisite quantity of wood, they throw the disfigured remains into the nearest river. The Ganges, being what they call a holy river, is more especially used for this purpose; and the bodies of the poor are frequently thrown into it without being burned at all. At Patnah, in times of great sickness, as many as four hundred have been seen floating past in a single day.

At one o'clock the cook-boat came close up to the budgerow; the kitmutgars brought the children's dinner on board, just as well dressed as if they had been on shore. They were very hungry, and of course considered it particularly good, from the novelty of having been cooked in a boat. In the afternoon they went to the little veranda, and watched the dandies, and looked out for alligators. On one sandbank they counted seven; they looked more like dry logs of wood than living creatures, and Alfred was inclined to think Bikoo was mistaken as to their being alligators at all, till he saw one of them, roused out of its sleep, scudding into the water as fast as possible. They were told that so high up the river as this, alligators were comparatively harmless; whereas in the lower parts near the sea they were dangerous and ferocious, sometimes carrying off cows from the banks, and sometimes, it is said, knocking the fishermen off their *dinghies*, or canoes, by a blow of their tail, and dragging them down into the deep. When our travellers passed a village, they were likewise amused by a whole herd of buffaloes coming down to bathe. Their unwieldy black bodies were soon entirely under water, and only their heads and horns were to be seen, with boys seated on them very comfortably.

It was not the least amusing business of the young travellers to watch the different kinds of cultivation that were carried on on the banks. Near Patnah there was a world of poppies, from which opium is obtained — for Patnah is the great opium district of Bengal. Lower down, the country is noted for its grain of all kinds, especially rice and maize, or Indian corn; and it was curious to see sentinels perched here and there on tall bamboo towers, driving away the birds with stones and incessant screams and shouts.

Evening came, the sun was set, and the day's work was done; a good resting-place for the night was found, and all the dandies and all the passengers of the five boats were on shore in a few minutes; and that shore, which half an hour before had been quite deserted, was now covered with a busy crowd. The boatmen were knocking pegs into the ground with heavy mallets, to make the boats fast to at night; others were lighting fires to cook their suppers; all the servants were busy in the same way. Alfred and Charles ran first to one group, then to another, quite delighted with this new scene; and when it was quite dark, they went and sat with their father and mother on the top of the budgerow.

"How pretty the fires look on the shore, mamma, and the boats on the river! This has been a very pleasant day. You thought we should get tired of the boat, but you see we are not."

"You have not had very long experience of the charms of a boat, and to-day all has been favourable. No one but a discontented peevish person could have complained. We have only stuck once upon a sandbank, the wind has been very moderate, and the heat not oppressive; no red ants to eat up our provisions, no cockroaches nor other disagreeable insects to eat ourselves: in fact I quite agree with you, my dear Alfred, this has been a very pleasant day; and this night is very beautiful, the air is so much cooler than on shore, that it is a great pleasure to sit here."

"How glad the dandies must be to get their food, they have worked so hard all day long!"

"Yes; if they had been Mussulman dandies, they would have cooked on board the boat; but as they are Hindoos, they will not eat anything cooked on the water. But it is time for you to go to bed; here is Bikoo coming for you; by and by the shore will be as deserted as we found it; all the fires will soon be out, the dandies will come on board and roll themselves up in their sheets and lie down on the deck, and we shall all sleep soundly, I hope, and be off again at daybreak."

The little boys did sleep soundly, notwithstanding the shouts of the chokeydars, or watchmen, and the screaming of the jackals, and were not even roused by the motion of the boat in the morning. They did not at first know where they were when their bearer awoke them to bathe and dress, which they did on the top of the boat, where they remained sitting for some time under the large chattah, till the outer cabin, in which they had slept on two small couches, was arranged for breakfast. For an hour or two afterwards, they employed themselves as they would have done on shore—reading and writing; and then Alfred said, "Come and sit down here, Charles, in our pleasant little nook, and I will teach you the moves at chess." The chess-board was spread out on the deck of the cabin, and they began setting up the men; but no sooner were they up, than they fell down again. After repeated attempts to set them up, Charles exclaimed, "Do look, mamma! The men will not stand up: how very troublesome! What is the reason?"

"Don't you feel the boat rocking? The wind has been rising the last half hour, and is now blowing so steadily against us, that I do not think we shall be able to get on much longer."

"Look, Alfred, here we are just opposite that old mosque which we were looking at after breakfast. I don't think we have moved the least bit since then; do you, mamma?"

"Yes, we have moved a little, but not above a quarter of a mile. The men have been toiling so long to so little purpose, that I expect them every minute to tie up the boat till the wind falls, which it will probably do about sunset. The motion of the boat is so very disagreeable, I shall be glad when they stop."

"It is getting worse every minute, mamma, and I really think we are going back again. There are all the things rolling off the table: this is very uncomfortable indeed. I wish you would desire them to stop."

"They have stopped already. They *were* going back, but it was only to get into this little creek, where we can tie up safely; and here we must remain till the wind moderates."

"Where are all the rest of the boats, mamma? I cannot see one of them."

"They are all on the opposite side of the river. I see them all quite safe."

"But it will soon be one o'clock. I hope the cook-boat will be able to come to us."

"I fear we must not expect the cook-boat till the wind falls, Alfred."

"Then if the wind does not fall soon, we shall be starved; for we have nothing to eat here, and there is nothing to be seen on shore."

"Do not alarm yourself; we all had a plentiful breakfast. It was lucky Buxsoo got us that fine Hilsa fish; and Charlie has found the tin box with the biscuits in it; and before they are all eaten up we may hope for a calm."

"I do not think the budgerow is so very pleasant to-day. I shall not be very sorry indeed when we get to Calcutta."

"This is only the second day, and we must take the evil with the good. Now the boat is steady, the chess-men will not fall: come and I will have a game with you. I will give you my bishop and my queen."

The chess-board was again produced, and the men did not fall; but the wind blew so violently, the Venetians were not sufficient to keep out the clouds of sand that penetrated them; and the coarse canvas curtains had also been let down outside, so that the cabin was dark; and even the game of chess failed to make the time pass pleasantly.

"Papa," at last said Alfred, "this is very uncomfortable indeed; the sand blows in so much, and it is so dark, I can scarcely see the men, and I cannot think about the game. Will you tell us a story? If we were listening to a nice long story, we should not think of the wind and the sand."

Their father did tell them a long story, and they listened attentively for nearly an hour. Just as he had finished, Alfred started up, exclaiming that he heard old Buxsoo's voice; and Buxsoo indeed it was, in a small dinghie, or canoe, belonging to the cook-boat. He said as long as the wind lasted the large boats could not move, so he had brought the children's curry and rice, and their father's and mother's too.

"It was very good of Buxsoo to come in the little boat," said Charles, as he sat very contentedly eating his dinner. "If the wind never stopped"——

"Oh, Charlie! Never stopped!"

"I mean, Alfred, if it had gone on blowing a great many days, we should have been starved; but now if Buxsoo can go backwards and forwards in the little boat, it does not signify if the wind lasts."

Towards evening the wind fell; and long after Alfred and Charles had fallen asleep, the dandies continued to row the boat. It was bright moonlight, and as they and the servants had eaten during the day, they were able to work very late; and when the little boys awoke the next morning, they were leaving Monghir, where there is nice shelter from the current of the river. They were just in time to get a peep at the immense fortress of this place, which their father told them was two miles square. The river is its ditch in front; and an artificial ditch, fifty feet broad, encloses it on the land side. Their eyes rested, however, with still greater interest upon a large and beautiful cemetery, with many tall and handsome monuments, which they saw just as they were leaving the town. The point of Jungheera came next, with the Faqueer's Rock before it, a hundred yards out in the river. On the summit of the point there is a Mohammedan tomb, where the people believe a great treasure is buried. The rock is covered with sculpture, except at the top, where there is a natural grove of trees surrounding a small temple. Here resides a kind of priest, who takes toll from the natives as they pass up or down the river, threatening them with shipwreck and all sorts of calamities if they refuse to comply with his demands. The travellers were told that this filthy and disgusting being, whom they saw sitting like a baboon upon the rock, and with scarcely more clothes on, was worth more than a million of English money; and that besides great possessions of land, he had a hundred thousand buffaloes.

At Bhangulpore they were still six hundred miles from the sea; and yet here this great river, in the rainy season, is eight miles broad. But so many changes have taken place in the channel, that at a point lower down, some little rocky islands which they admired very much, with their crown of beautiful trees, were, not a great many years before, at a considerable distance from the water. After passing Bhangulpore, they were amused with the sight of a fleet of boats carrying to market cargoes of live fish, kept in wells communicating with the river. At the outlets of the streams running into this part of the Ganges the quantities of fish are enormous. The hamlets on the banks were also a pleasing sight, with their cows coming home in the evening, each with an iron bell round its neck, the sound of which wafted over the river was very agreeable. Jungle fowl likewise were frequently seen; and although they are merely cocks and hens in a wild state, the cock is a much more splendid fellow than was ever seen in a poultry-yard.

They now passed some wild-looking hills, where Alfred was told by his father there were plenty of tigers, leopards, and wild hogs, and where even the rarer rhinoceros may be seen sometimes coming down to wallow in the river.

"Hollo!" cried Alfred; "there is one now—two—three—a dozen—or more!"

"Look again," said his father quietly.

"I do! And oh, papa, do you not also see these great black horns and wild staring eyes above the surface of the water near the edge of the river?"

"Yes; and they are old acquaintances of yours, although the rhinoceros has put them out of your head. They are tame buffaloes, which lie in that way for hours enjoying the coolness of the water."

He had scarcely spoken, when some men came down the bank driving more buffaloes before them, and presently those in the river raised up their huge bodies, and all stood together in a crowd, looking straight towards our travellers' vessel, as if meditating a visit.

"What are they going to do?" cried Alfred, watching them with intense curiosity. "I declare they are coming to us!" And at the words the men screamed and shouted, and the buffaloes dashed into the river, followed by their drivers, who appeared to have the herd divided among them, each laying hold of the tail of one of the largest of the animals. The children at first hung back, uncertain as to what their object might be; but when told that this was a common way of crossing the river, they leant over the side as the cavalcade passed, and clapped their hands with delight. At another place, where the river was at least a thousand yards wide, they saw a poor pariah dog crossing in the same manner; but this was perhaps an unusual spectacle, for it attracted the curiosity of a crowd of crows, which assailed him with wing and beak during the whole of his passage.

The incessant tumbling of the porpoises around them, at first amusing, was at last seen with indifference; but not so the motions of the pelicans, which always kept exactly out of shot range, although they never gave themselves the trouble to go farther. At the confluence of the different streams with the Ganges, these birds were seen standing upon the sandbanks in assemblies of nearly a hundred, apparently holding a consultation as to the state of the fishing. At these places the water seemed perfectly alive with fish; and Alfred and Charles could sometimes get a glance at them swimming in myriads just under the surface. On several occasions they saw the natives employed in spearing turtle, which put them in mind of the stories they had read of whale-fishing. Paddling along came a light dinghie, or canoe, with a man standing in the bow holding a spear poised in his hand, having a cord attached to it. Presently an unfortunate turtle puts up his head to breathe, and in an instant he is transfixed with the light weapon and drawn into the boat. But the fishermen now find themselves among a shoal of mullet, and they must have recourse to another weapon. This is a long light bamboo with a number of sharp spikes at the end, which, on being darted into the shoal, is sure to spit some of its number. These are the most delicious fish of the Ganges, and are always seen swimming against the current with their heads above the water, and looking very like a company of serpents.

The village of Rajmahal was next passed, with its ruined palace, once the residence of Sultan Sujah, one of the brothers of Aurungzebe. But the children were more interested by the stories they heard here of the changes of the river, and the conduct, during the time of the inundations, of the poor people who inhabit the banks. Sometimes whole villages are flooded, the houses and elevated spots looking like islands in a sea. But for all that, the inhabitants will rarely leave their houses, but sit quietly on the house-tops, waiting for whatever the event may be. Sometimes the magistrate, seeing that the infatuated creatures will perish without his aid, sends a police force to fetch them away in boats.

"But when they are fetched away," said

Alfred, "they of course never go back to so dangerous a place?"

"The moment the waters subside they return to repair their huts, and inhabit them anew. This is just the way with the snakes and rats, which, when the flood is coming in, dispute with the human inhabitants every inch of dry ground they can find. Many of them are of course drowned or killed; but when the immediate danger is over, there are as many snakes and rats about the village as before. It is said that the Hindoo women are still more remarkable than the men for this singular love of home."

The large but ruinous city of Dhacca, in the neighbourhood of their route, but too far off to be seen, excited much curiosity; and Alfred was greatly interested by the account his mother gave him of the muslins for which the place was once famous.

"Thousands of families," said she, "inhabited the suburbs, whose business was weaving; and such was the delicacy of this manufacture, that they were obliged to work in pits, so as to be sheltered from the sun. But even this precaution was not enough, for they could only continue at the loom while the dew was on the ground, as the heat at other times reached them in sufficient force to destroy their gossamer-like threads. All this is now at an end, for the handlooms of Dhacca could not stand the competition of the machinery of Manchester."

"What a pity!" cried Alfred. "And are there no weavers there now at all?"

"Yes, there are still some; and by giving a commission, I could get a very delicate article made—that is, if I could afford it. But it would cost me a hundred and fifty rupees for ten yards. Shawl scarfs, however, are worked very beautifully with flossed silk, and at reasonable prices. As for the deserted pits, they are now filled with stagnant water, and render the place very unhealthy."

The weather now became very boisterous; and what was worse, they found the mouth of the Jelinghy, which would have been their shortest way to the Hoogly, was choked with sand; and the night they arrived there, what was usually the channel in which the boats sail was now so dry, that the children employed themselves picking their way across it without wetting their shoes. They forgot their disappointment in the novelty of this amusement, till they were driven into the boat by very heavy rain, which fell all night, and every one hoped the channel would be a little deeper the next day. But that day, and the next, and the next, it was impossible to move the boats. The provisions now really began to fall short, and altogether the prospect was so dreary, that Alfred was not ashamed to confess he was quite tired of the voyage. Four days they had passed with their boat fastened under a high hot bank swarming with mosquitoes. On the fifth, old Buxsoo said he was sure the water was deep enough for the budgerow. The boatmen were not sure, but they were willing to try; but all their efforts were useless to move it more than half a quarter of a mile, and again they stuck as fast as ever.

"What will become of us!" exclaimed Charles, after all hopes of success were abandoned. "We have been here in the jungles such a long time, I wish we were safe back again in our own house. I liked the boat very well at first, but I am quite tired of it now. Do you think we shall ever get to Calcutta, mamma?"

"I hope so. Do not look so miserable: that will not help us. We must now try another plan: as we cannot go in the budgerow, we must leave it and all our large boats here till the river rises, and we must cross this shallow part in a small boat. A mile farther on there is deep water, and a good many large native boats—unfortunately no budgerows; but we must try and get a *patello*, that is, a large and light boat which draws little water, to take us the rest of the voyage."

All was now bustle and confusion removing whatever was thought necessary for comfort from the budgerow to the small boat. Alfred was as busy as possible, and therefore quite happy; and little Charles did his best to help. They did not get on board their new vessel till near sunset. It was large, but looked very different from the light, clean, well-arranged one they had left; and as soon as Alfred saw it, he exclaimed, "What an uncomfortable place! There is no division from one end of the boat to the other, and I am sure we shall tumble down if we attempt to walk on these rough bamboos; and there are no windows, only mats all round; and this dark low roof; and"——

"Stop, dear Alfred; find out all the good qualities of this ark of ours instead of the bad: we must do the best we can for to-night, and to-morrow we will try and make it more comfortable. We might be much worse off: it is a fine night, and a bright moon, and it is a comfort to think we shall not be stuck fast in the sand to-morrow."

"I don't think we shall be any more comfortable: we are all in the dark: we cannot see to do a single thing."

"We do not want to see anything just now; we want to make haste to get to Calcutta; and if we can pass a quiet night, and start early to-morrow morning, we need not complain because we cannot look about us."

A quiet night, however, they did not pass; for soon after the little boys were in bed, a thick black cloud covered the moon, the wind rose, and the rain fell heavily, pouring in through all parts of the thatch of which the roof was composed. Alfred jumped out of his bed as fast as he could, into which the water soaked, and began a loud lamentation and complaint, supposing he was the only sufferer. In the midst of his distress, Bikoo and the rest of the bearers came running in with chattahs, or umbrellas, in their hands, under which he and his brother were obliged to sit, and where their father and mother joined them, whilst the servants endeavoured to discover dry places for the beds, which was a work of time. The scene was so ludicrous, that all Alfred's wailings were turned into shouts of laughter, which did not cease till he had been some time in bed. The next day they were often tempted to complain, but on the whole they bore their confinement as well as most other active little boys would have done. Unfortunately the boat was not only inconvenient, but a bad one in every respect; and it was joyous news when Buxsoo reported that they were close to an empty budgerow, which could be hired for the rest of the voyage. The bargain was soon made; and here was another change, but a much pleasanter one than the last.

"Well, papa," said Alfred when they were all established comfortably in their new quarters, "this is better than our last boat: we shall not want chattahs to-night. But I cannot help laughing whenever I think of our sitting there with the rain pattering on our chattahs, and the bearers running about to find a dry place; when, just as they thought they had found one, down came a great plump of water on their heads, and Charlie looked so melancholy; but none of us need be melancholy now. How beautiful and green the country looks! At the mouth of the Jelinghy it was nothing but sand; but here it is so green and fresh, and we can look out so delightfully. We could see nothing in that dismal dark patello. I hope now we shall get to Calcutta without any more adventures."

"I hope we shall too; but if we meet with any difficulties, we must endeavour to meet them with good-humour. I foresee one trial we shall have, for we have no more bread nor flour; but as we have rice, we cannot starve; so we are not much to be pitied."

The next day, notwithstanding the comforts of the budgerow, poor little Charles was very ill indeed, and then Alfred became peevish too. They were so ill, that they could take no pleasure in what was passing around them. Their father and mother were very anxious to get to the end of their voyage, for they had no proper food for their sick boys. The poor little fellows were very patient, and did not complain; but Alfred could not help saying he wished to be in a house once more.

"When first I came on the river, papa, I

expected so much pleasure, and to be so happy, and to like the boat so much; but I do not think one of the pleasures I expected has come to pass."

"But a great many you did not expect have come; and when we are all safe and well in Calcutta, it will be a great amusement to look back upon all our *little* misfortunes; and I hope we shall also look back with heartfelt thankfulness that we have had no *great* misfortunes, my dear boy, but so many mercies and comforts."

Whilst they were talking, they heard a small boat paddle up to theirs, and Buxsoo soon appeared in the cabin with a tray full of fine ripe mangoes, and a basket in which was some sweet fresh bread. It was nearly four weeks since they had seen fresh bread, and even the languid looks of the little boys brightened up at the sight of it; and Alfred said, "Why, papa, I did not know we were near any town. Where are we?—where did this bread come from?"

It had come from a gentleman who was an indigo factor, who had seen their boats passing when he was out on his elephant; and as he knew from the state of the river they must have been some time in the jungles, he had the kindness and consideration to send them some new-baked bread and fruit.

"How very kind of him to send these things to us!" said Alfred. "This was a pleasure we did not expect."

"No, we certainly did not expect this; and I hear more good tidings—the dandies are saying to each other that we shall get to Kishnaghur to-night, and then we shall soon be at our journey's end, for the tides reach to Kishnaghur."

The next day the little invalids were much better, and able to sit in the early morning on the top of the boat. They were quite delighted with the beauty of Kishnaghur. The cocoa-nut-trees were new to them, for they do not grow in the upper provinces. The banks of the river were no longer deserted; before one village was out of sight, another appeared. Then they reached Culna, with its busy crowded *ghauts*, or landing-places; then Hoogly, with its handsome houses, belonging to rich natives; then Burrackpore, with its beautiful park, large cantonments, and Government House. And on the last day of their fifth week they anchored off Chandpaul Ghaut, all very glad to reach Calcutta.

CALCUTTA.

Calcutta is situated about a hundred miles from the sea, on the east bank of the Hoogly, a branch of the Ganges. The length of the town is about six miles along the bank of the river. Calcutta is not an ancient city; it has been built chiefly by the English, who have here erected a large and strong fort, called Fort-William. Properly speaking, there are two towns—the native town behind, and the English town in front. The native or Black Town, as it is called, is a mean and confused place—crooked streets, huts of earth baked in the sun, or made of twisted bamboos, ruinous brick bazaars or markets, pools of dirty water, cocoa-nut-trees, and little gardens, with some gaudy large houses, the residences of the wealthy natives.

The new or English town consists generally of fine white buildings, and the appearance of the tall and stately houses, with spacious verandas, is very noble. The principal public building is Government House, where the Governor-General resides, and holds his court. It occupies a pleasant situation near the river, which is about a mile wide at Calcutta.

The appearance of the streets and the people, particularly in the old town, always amuses strangers from its novelty. The account which Bishop Heber gives of what he saw is so correct, that I shall transcribe it. "Imagine," says he, "a crowd of people in the street beyond anything to be seen even in London, some dressed in tawdry silks and brocades, more in white cotton garments, and most of all black and naked, except a scanty covering round the waist, besides figures of religious mendicants, with no clothing but their long hair and beards in elf-locks, their faces painted white or yellow, their beads in one ghastly lean hand, and the other stretched out like a bird's claw to receive donations; marriage processions, with the bride in a covered chair, and the bridegroom on horseback, so swathed round with garlands as hardly to be seen; tradesmen sitting on the ground in the midst of their different commodities, and old men, lookers-on, perched naked as monkeys on the flat roofs of the houses; carts drawn by oxen, and driven by wild-looking men with thick sticks, so unmercifully used, as to undeceive perfectly all our notions of Brahminical humanity; attendants with silver maces, pressing through the crowd before the carriage of some great man or other; no women seen except of the lowest class, and even these with heavy silver ornaments on their dusky arms and ankles; while coaches, covered up close with red cloth, are seen conveying the inmates of the neighbouring seraglios to take what is called 'the air;' a constant creaking of cart wheels, which are never greased in India, a constant clamour of voices, and an almost constant thumping and jingling of drums, cymbals, &c. in honour of their deities; and add to all this a villanous smell of garlic, rancid cocoa-nut oil, sour butter, and stagnant ditches, and you will understand the sounds, sights, and smells of what is called the ' Black Town' of Calcutta. The singularity of this spectacle is best and least offensively enjoyed on a noble quay which

Lord Hastings built along the shore of the river, where the vessels of all forms and sizes—Arab, Indian, Malay, American, English; the crowds of Brahmins and other Hindoos washing and saying their prayers; the lighted tapers which, towards sunset, they throw in, and the broad bright stream which sweeps by them, guiltless of their impiety, and unconscious of their homage —afford a scene such as no European, and few Asiatic cities, can at all parallel in interest and singularity."

Alfred, to whom everything was new, was greatly amused with Calcutta, and a residence of three months in it passed away very swiftly. He was taken to see the Fort, Bishop's College, and the Botanical Gardens and Government House.

"Do you know, mamma," said he one day, "I was not disappointed in Government House, as I was in the palace of Rajmahal. I think it looks very handsome, with the large house in the middle, and the four smaller houses joining on to the corners. But why did they not build one very large house instead of the four wings?"

"I suppose it was thought that the present

plan would be the coolest, for now there is always a current of air passing through each of these smaller buildings; but if it had been one compact mass, it would have been impossible to have obtained that refreshment."

" Ay, I suppose that is the reason: I did not think of that. The marble hall in Government House is very grand; and the gray marble floor, and the marble pillars all along the sides, with the busts of the twelve Cæsars on them, and the gilding on the roof, are all beautiful."

" What do you think I like best of all about Government House?" said Charles.

" I do not know. Is it the long long flight of steps, and the portico outside?" said Alfred.

" No, not the steps; but it *is* outside the House."

" It is the arched gateways, and the lions on them—I like them very much too."

" No, it is not the gateways and the lions. It is the quantities of adjutants, the tall birds that stand on one leg, with the other tucked up, all round the parapet—Isn't it parapet, mamma?" (His mother smiled, and nodded)— " with their long ugly beaks, and their pouches hanging down from their breasts, and their grisly heads; they look so very strange. Papa told me they were very useful, and picked up all sorts of dirty things that are to be found in the streets. I suppose there are no adjutants in London?"

"You are quite right in supposing so."

"Is Calcutta like London?"

"No. In the first place, Calcutta cannot be compared to London in size; for in an evening drive, you know we can go all round Calcutta; but it would require half a day to get round London. Then in Calcutta *all* the houses are white, and plastered to look like stone, and the lofty pillars supporting the spacious verandas give them a very handsome and imposing appearance; and then they are all detached one from the other, each standing in its own compound, full of trees and large beautiful flowering shrubs; whilst in London it is one long street after another of brick houses, dingy from smoke, with the doors opening on the streets, and"——

"But there are some houses here opening on the street, and all joined together."

"Yes, a few. The row of houses called the Writers' Buildings, on one side of Tank Square,

are all joined together, as you call it, but even these are not like the houses in London. Tank Square is much larger than any of the squares there, but not nearly so pretty as many of them. There is one peculiarity in Calcutta which you will not meet with in London—I mean the miserable rows of native huts that are to be seen even close to the finest houses, and in the handsomest streets. They not only look very ill, but they are very dangerous. Do you not remember when the bazaar close to our house was on fire?"

"Oh yes, and we were afraid it would reach us. I wonder they do not build better houses; but there are some grand native houses along the Circular Road, mamma."

"Yes, there are some very handsome native residences in the Circular Road, but these belong to rich people."

"I am always glad when it is not too dusty to drive along the Circular Road; I like to look at the cocoa-nut-trees and the bamboo topes, all spangled over with fire-flies, and the Mohammedan burying-grounds with the lamps in the tombs."

"Well, Charles, I don't care much for the

Circular Road; I like driving through Fort-William much better—clatter, clatter, clatter over the three drawbridges, and through the gateways; and then inside everything looks in such nice order, and the large piles of cannon balls, of all sizes, heaped up in such exact pyramids, and the large guns: it is all so different from the fort at Monghir."

"Which was only the ruin of a fort, my dear Alfred; but in Fort-William everything is in the highest order. I have been told it is considered impregnable; the only defect is its size, and more men would be required to garrison it than food could be easily procured for; and there is not a plentiful supply of good water. But we must hope the days are passed when it will be required as a place of defence."

"I wish, mamma, you could go with us to see the Mint. Papa is going to take us again; and if you are stronger, you can go with us and see the furnaces, and the large wedges of silver, and the great giant scissors chopping them into pieces; and then the rupees being made, and then stamped. Don't you think you can go, mamma?"

"No, Charles, I am afraid I must be contented with admiring the handsome stone building outside; for the heat and the confusion and the noise inside would be too great."

"And I am afraid, mamma, you will not be able to go and see the Bhurra Bazaar. You cannot think what a curious place it is—such narrow little lanes, with little crowded shops on each side, and such numbers of natives pushing, and crushing, and all talking together, and asking us to buy something, and we could see nothing to buy but those shells we brought you. The bearers said the good shops were over these, and the men in them had silks and satins, and even jewels of all kinds to sell; but we did not want any, and so papa would not go up and give them the trouble of unpacking all their chests merely for our amusement. The China Bazaar is not nearly such a crushing place, and the shops are much larger, and all the things they have to sell are laid out on tables, and in glass-cases, just like the European shops. You can go there, mamma, when you want to buy anything; for there is plenty of room for the palanquin to go along, and there are all sorts of things to be bought; so when you want anything, we will take you to the China Bazaar."

"I have no doubt you will be very happy to escort me; and when the weather is cooler, you shall have that honour."

"And when the weather is cooler, will you be able to go to the Botanical Gardens and spend a whole day, and take our tiffin, and have it out of doors under the large banyan-trees? I want so very much to go there and see the pond with the fish in it that come when they are called, and eat the bread that is thrown into them."

"Who told you of these wonderful fish?"

"Charlotte and Mary told us. They were there last cold season, and it is *quite* true about the fish, for they saw them; and they say there are so many beautiful climbing-plants, and curious trees—the nutmeg-tree and the sago palm; and the walks are so shady, that they remained in the gardens the whole day. Oh do pray go! Will you, mamma?"

"Yes, I should like very much to go; and we can spend part of the day with our kind friends at Bishop's College, and see the fine library, and attend the service in its beautiful chapel before we return in the evening."

"Bishop's College is for teaching native Christians—is it not, mamma?"

"Yes, my dear."

"And some day papa says he is going to take us to see the Hindoo college, where there are a great many native boys—three hundred, I think—and they learn English, and mathematics, and astronomy, and all about electricity and geology, and such things; and papa says they know quite as much as many well-educated boys of their own age in England."

"The Hindoo college is for boys who are rich, and whose parents are able to pay for their education. But I will take you to Mrs Wilson's school for poor little native girls, who cannot pay for learning, but are so poor, they are glad to be paid for being taught, which she does, that she may encourage them to learn. And if they profit by her teaching and good example, the time may come when their parents will think it desirable to educate their daughters as well as their sons, though grand colleges will not be required for this purpose. They may give them teachers, and this I hope they will do."

THE SHIP.

The carriage was at the door, and Alfred and Charles were soon seated in it by the side of their father; and the coachman was ordered to drive to the Strand.

"Then, papa, the ship is close to the shore, and not in the middle of the stream? And we shall not be obliged to have a dinghie to go out to her? I am rather sorry for that, for I am afraid the ship will not be a very large one."

"It is not a very large one, but it is the first opportunity that has offered since we came to Calcutta of showing you a ship, and therefore I was glad to take advantage of it. But here we are at the ghât."

The captain received them with great kindness, and was anxious to show them every part of his vessel, and to tell the names and explain the uses of the various ropes. Then he showed them the capstan, and the binnacle, and the wheel. Though he explained with great clearness, they were rather bewildered and a little disappointed; and they could not take in so much at once. The extreme order and neatness astonished them: even the decks were not only clean, but shining. They had expected to see a crowd of sailors on board, but there were very few; and though very unlike the dandies of their boats, they were not like what they had fancied sailors to be.

After they had seen everything on deck, the captain took them into his cabin, which was as clean and orderly as the rest of the ship. On the table, in the middle of it, some cake and preserved fruits and wine were prepared for his guests, of which he very kindly pressed them to partake, telling them he had brought the cake all the way from Boston in New England, and that they would find it quite fresh. Alfred and Charles thanked him very much, but said they would rather not eat any of the cake; but they inquired with one voice if those beautiful rosy apples on the table had come from America too.

"Yes," said the captain; "they came from Boston. But did you never see apples before, that you think so much of them?"

"We have seen a few," said Alfred, "that men sometimes brought wrapped up in cotton; but they looked pale and withered, not fresh and rosy like these; but then they had come a long way—all the way overland from Persia."

"These did not come overland to be sure," said the captain; "but Boston is farther off from Calcutta than Persia."

"Then how can you have kept them so fresh? Perhaps the sea air has kept them so?"

"No; I kept as much of the sea air from them as possible."

"Then did you wrap them in cotton too, sir?"

"No; I did not wrap them in cotton to keep them warm, I put them with something to keep them cool—something very cold."

"Very cold," said Charles—"very cold! What could that be?"

"Did you ever hear of ice?"

"Yes; we have heard of ice, but we have never seen any. How did you get the ice? And how did you keep it? Did it not melt and turn to water? Did you keep the apples in the ice? Have you any now in your ship, sir? If you have any, pray do let us see it," said Alfred with great eagerness. "I would rather see it than all the things you have shown us."

The good-natured captain was very much amused at Alfred's impetuosity, and said, "You have asked me so many questions, I do not know which was the first; but I think somewhere about the last was, if I had any ice now? Yes; and if you and your brother will each take an apple, and tell me if it is not much better than a mangoe, I will show you the ice; for we are just going to open the hold, and to be very busy."

Alfred and Charles followed the captain with eager curiosity, and were not now disappointed. They saw several large blocks of ice, as clear as glass, lifted out of the ship's hold by means of pulleys, and carried away on shore as fast as possible, to be placed in an ice-house prepared for them. The blocks of ice were swung to a pole, which two men carried; they waited till past sunset before they opened the hold, to avoid the heat as much as they could, and the hold was closed again as soon as possible.

"Oh, papa, did you know before we came that we should see the ice?"

"Yes I did."

"And did mamma know too?"

"Yes; but she said nothing about it, as she did not wish to *bribe* you to do what you knew to be right."

"I am so very glad we came; but I am afraid the ice will melt away in the ice-house."

"I am afraid some will melt, though every pains has been taken to make this temporary ice-house as air-tight as possible; and it will only be opened late at night, or very early in the morning, to sell it to those who may wish to buy."

"Will you buy some, papa? But if you do, what use can you make of it?"

"Yes, Charles, we shall buy some; for we can use it to cool the water, and the wine, and the butter, instead of saltpetre."

"I cannot think how the captain kept it from melting on such a long voyage. Do you know, papa?"

"He says a great deal has melted, but he took every possible precaution to exclude the air; the inside of the hold was lined with bark, and as soon as it was quite full, the top was fastened down, and not opened till they arrived here. These large blocks were not so likely to melt as smaller pieces would have been; and for a first experiment, this has been a very successful one."

"Do you know, papa, how they get such very large blocks of ice?"

"Yes; they have ponds on purpose in the neighbourhood of Boston, which are kept pure and clean, and used only for making ice. The winter is always sufficiently severe in New England to turn the water into firm ice; and then, by means of machines, these large blocks are cut. For many years, ice has been sent from the United States to the West Indies; but we never expected to see it brought to India. Even in the neighbourhood of Calcutta, there are very thin plates of ice obtained by evaporation; but in Upper India, it is procured in the cold season by the exposure of shallow jars filled with water, and covered with straw, in sufficient quantities to last during the rest of the year. It is too dear, however, to be of use to any but the rich, as an annual subscription entitling to a daily supply costs thirty pounds. When an entertainment is given, it is customary for the guests to send their own ice; and sometimes the family will abstain from drawing their allowance for several days, so that a good quantity may be due to them on the morning of the feast. However, it is now getting quite dark, and we must say good-by to the captain, who has been so very kind and attentive to us."

The captain had been too busy for some time to speak to them; but now he found leisure to shake hands with his young visitors, and said good-humouredly, "Well, my little fellows, you looked disappointed at first with my ship; but what do you think of her cargo? Do you like apples as well as mangoes?"

"We have quite forgotten to eat our apples: we have been so much astonished and amused with the ice, that we never thought of them," said Alfred.

"Well, you must come and see me again, and then you will have had time to make up your minds. Good-night. Look under the seat of your carriage, and see if there is any ice there."

The boys and their father shook hands with the captain, and wished him good-night too, and begged he would come and see them as soon as he could.

"What a very good-natured man that captain

is!" said Charles, as soon as they were in the carriage: "he was so kind and so merry. But what could he mean by ice under the seat? Oh there is no ice, but some most beautiful apples! I am so glad! I intended to take mine to mamma; but I think there are some finer and larger ones here than ours."

"She will never be able to guess what we have got for her. She knows about the ship and the ice, but not about the apples," said Alfred. "Here we are at home: let me run up stairs to her and ask her to guess what we have got."

His mother was sitting in the veranda enjoying the cool air by moonlight. The day had been very hot; but she was refreshed, and was very glad to hear the merry voices of her little boys as they ran up to her. She asked if they were pleased with the ship?

"No, not nearly so much as we expected to be with the ship itself: it was so small—not so big as some of the cotton boats we used to see coming down the Ganges; but the captain was very kind, and I wish he would come and see us soon."

"I hope he will," said Charles; "he told

me he had some children in America. I wish we could send them some mangoes when he goes back, but we have no ice to pack them in. I daresay they would like mangoes as much as we do apples."

Whilst they were eating their supper, they continued their observations, and fell asleep talking of the ship, the sailors, the captain, apples, and ice.

The next morning, soon after they had set off for their ride, and long before sunrise, they met one of their father's servants carrying something in a basket, which was wrapped up in a piece of coarse thick baize.

"What have you got there, Rajoo?" said Alfred. "Are you returning from the bazaar already?"

Rajoo said he had not been to the bazaar, it was too early; but he had been to the ice-house for ice. He had got some, which was put in a small basket, and that basket was wrapped up in straw, and outside the straw was this thick woollen cloth, folded several times. He was desired particularly to exclude the air, and to be at home before sunrise, and put it in the house of the aubdar, or servant who has charge of the water for drinking; for it was cooler than any other place. So he went home, and the boys continued their ride; but returned earlier than usual, that they might inquire how the ice was to be used in cooling the butter for breakfast.

A few small nobs, as clear as crystal, were put round the butter, and it became hard and firm. The ice did not last very long this first day, for every one that came to the house was to be astonished with it; and before the children's dinners, it was all melted except two little pieces, which cooled a tumbler of water for each of them.

The afternoon was particularly hot and oppressive—the punkah gave very little relief: every one longed for the time when the doors and windows might be opened, and they might go out to drive, or ride, or walk. Alfred and Charles were so hot, and languid, and weary, they could not even play, and sat talking to their mother of the still wonderful ice.

"Will you tell us, mamma, about the ice that is made even in this hot Calcutta?"

"It is in very thin sheets, scarcely thicker than writing-paper; but it is not made exactly in Calcutta, but at Chinsura, and there only in the cold season, when the wind is dry, and blows from the west. You know we passed Chinsura as we came down to Calcutta the last day we were on the river."

"But if it can be made at Chinsura, which is so near, why can it not be made here instead of getting it all the way from America?"

"I cannot explain to you why it cannot be made in Calcutta, but I can imagine many reasons—for one, the vicinity of the salt-water lake. I have never seen the ice fields at Chinsura, but I have been told they are cut in ridges. The spaces between these ridges are nearly filled with straw—on this straw porous earthen saucers are placed full of water (you know porous means full of pores, or very small holes). Early in the morning a very thin sheet of ice is found, which is collected, carefully packed up, and sent down to Calcutta, where it arrives as black as jet, instead of the beautiful clear crystal lumps we have had to-day."

"Shall we see ice when we go to England?"

"Certainly, during the winter; but the ice which is formed on English lakes and rivers is not so cold and compact as that of North

America, and it is therefore more easily melted, and of less value. The American ice is also the purest."

"Do you know, mamma, I wanted Bikoo and all the bearers to put a little bit of ice in their mouths to feel what a strange feeling it is, but they would not? I think they were very foolish. They said they should lose caste if they put the very least bit to the tip of their tongues, as if the ice could hurt them. Don't you think they were very foolish?"

"No, I cannot say I think them so very foolish: they were not afraid of the ice hurting them, but they were afraid of committing a sin by tasting it."

"But you know, mamma, they would not commit a sin," replied Alfred.

"Yes, *I* know it, and so do you, but they have not been taught better; and you should respect them if they are obedient to the laws they consider binding: instead of laughing at them, you should imitate them."

"What! in not eating ice, mamma?"

"No, not exactly," said his mother; "but in dreading to do wrong. We have a pure and holy law to guide us, if we would but obey it as carefully as the poor Hindoos obey what they are taught to respect. We should try to be thankful for the light that has been given us, and not despise the natives around us because they are in darkness."

"But why has light not been given to them?" inquired Alfred.

"My dear little boy," said his mother solemnly, "the wisest man in all the world could not answer this. We only know we are all children of one good and merciful God, and He has seen fit to make this distinction for a *season*. We know that God is *love*, let us trust all to *Him*. We cannot help pitying the natives around us; we should pray for them, and we should endeavour to teach them the value of our superior knowledge by our good conduct. But, my dear boy, never on any account insult them by laughing at them, or calling them foolish for abstaining from what appears a sin to them:—think of this. And now they are coming to open the doors and windows, and by the time you are ready, we may go out."

The windows were opened, but still the heat seemed more than usually oppressive; and just as the children were dressed, the bearers ran hastily into the room and shut the windows as quickly as possible, for a great storm was coming: and indeed before they were all firmly fastened, the storm had come, and the wind blew furiously. Clouds of dust darkened the air, and covered the chairs, tables, and all the furniture, as it forced its way through the closely-barred windows. In a few minutes the thunder roared, and the forked lightning flashed vividly: the sky was quite overcast, but no rain fell.

Alfred and Charles ran into the sitting-room to their father and mother; for though they were accustomed to storms, yet they never remembered such a dreadful one as this. The thunder seemed louder and the lightning more vivid every moment.

"How glad I am we are not in the ship, as we were last night! Do you think we are quite safe here, mamma?" said Charles.

"We are as safe here as anywhere, my dear; we cannot escape from the storm. All we can do is to remain quiet and trustful till it has passed over. Such a storm as this is awful, but it need not be frightful. Hark!

the rain is pouring down now, and the wind is not quite so tremendous."

"What will the poor captain do in this storm, papa? He will not be able to take any ice out of the ship this evening. How dreadful such a storm must be at sea! Were you ever in a storm at sea, papa?"

"Yes, I have been in several. Once the gale lasted for a whole week. The ship was a very fine large one, and was very high out of the water; still all the windows on the poop were obliged to be shut, and what are called the dead-lights, or shutters, closely fastened, to prevent the sea beating them in. The waves washed over the deck continually, and were sometimes higher than the tall masts of the good ship. We were coming round the Cape of Good Hope, which was at first called by its discoverer Diaz the Cape of Storms. The grampuses were sporting about in the waves, and the turmoil of the waters seemed as delightful to them as it was distressing to us. We were all most uncomfortable; everything wet inside as well as outside the ship; no light in the cabins but from our lamps; and the furniture constantly breaking loose from its fastenings, and rolling about the deck. But though even the captain confessed it was a very stiff gale, he could always manage the ship, and I never felt in so much danger as I have done on the Ganges in the rainy season. The captain knew how to command, and the men how to obey, and therefore we felt confidence in them; but the crews of budgerows are often mere coolies, and know nothing about boats, or what to do in the time of danger. Once I remember"——

"Oh what a flash! but the thunder is not so near," said Alfred. "Go on, papa; tell us about the storm on the river."

"Well, once when your mother and I were going up the country, we were sitting in the afternoon in our budgerow waiting for dinner. A fine breeze sprung up, which was in our favour. Every sail was set, for we had been becalmed several days, and we were anxious to reach Patnah. We went on very pleasantly, dashing through the water for about half an hour, thinking of no danger, when old Buxsoo— he was not old then—rushed into the cabin, and without speaking, seized the carving-knife from the table and ran out again. I followed him immediately; but before I reached the deck, he had cut the rope which fastened the sail to the mast, and it fell down, and flapped uselessly against it. We were safe; but close to us a very large native boat, full of passengers, and which, like us, had been carrying too much sail, went over, and every soul on board was drowned."

"Oh how dreadful! But there is the thunder again. What a crash! Could you not help the poor people, papa?"

"No, my boy, it was quite impossible; and if Buxsoo had not had the presence of mind to cut the ropes, we should have gone too. The mangie had not sense enough to tell the dandies what to do, and they would probably not have understood him, or been able to obey his commands, if he had given any. We were very much distressed that we could be of no use to the poor sufferers; but you must remember how rapidly and impetuously the river ran past the fort at Monghir, how swiftly the boats were carried down by the stream, how completely and rapidly the villages on its banks were washed away, and how impossible it was for a boat to stem the torrent, unless it had a strong wind in its favour."

"Yes, papa, I remember quite well. How

fortunate it was that Buxsoo knew what to do!"

"It was indeed: but on board ship, no one would think of directing what was to be done; they would trust all to the captain and his officers. But there has been no thunder for some time, and the wind has moderated, so we may order the windows to be opened."

The windows were opened, and a cool, almost cold air blew in, so refreshing after the oppressive heat of the day, that every one felt thankful for the storm, though it had been so severe while it lasted. The ground, which had been so hard and dry an hour before, was now in many places under water; the parched shrubs were bright and green; the adjutants clattered their long beaks, as they sat on the branches of the trees, now bending beneath the abundant moisture; the frogs croaked loudly and merrily in the swollen rivulets which were formed in the garden—all nature seemed refreshed. The children, no longer oppressed by the heat, ran up and down the veranda, also rejoicing in the change.

"And now," said Charles, "as the rain is over, the good-natured little captain can begin to unload his ship. Oh, mamma, shall we see another ship?"

"I hope you will. There are no ships here now that will sail at the season to suit us; but by and by we shall find one that will take you at least some distance on your way to England."

"And are we really and truly going to England, and you and papa with us? Have you *quite* determined to go, papa?"

"I have not quite decided, Alfred; but you are both now getting too old to remain in India; and I hope by this time next year we shall all have taken leave of Calcutta for a season, have safely passed the Cape of Storms, and be happily settled at home."

THE VOYAGE HOME.

It was a busy and a happy interval with Alfred and his brother when the time was at last fixed for their leaving India. Their parents, too, became more anxious; for the boys were about the age when the climate has an unfavourable effect upon the young constitution, which requires to grow and strengthen in the breezes of Europe. It turned out, unfortunately, that their father's affairs did not permit him to go with them; but he was very willing to sacrifice for a time the company of his children, for the probability of his finding them in a few years great, strong, well-educated lads, fit to bear, if necessary, the heats of India, and make their way in the world. Their mother's health had already suffered; and it was determined, both on their account and her own, that she should take them to England, and see them fairly established in their new home.

By this time a great change had taken place in the manner of travelling between India and England. It was no longer necessary to go round by the Cape of Good Hope—a voyage of five or six months; for a steamer had already begun to ply between Bombay and Suez, at the head of the Red Sea, and passengers went from the latter place across the desert to Alexandria, and from thence in another steamer down the Mediterranean to England. This is called the "overland route," on account of the desert between the two seas, which breaks the voyage. Many persons still prefer coming home by the Cape; but those who like to see strange sights and strange countries choose the overland route. This was the way selected for Alfred and Charles; and you may suppose our young wanderers were not a little proud of their expected travels, when they were shown on the map that they were to visit Arabia and Egypt, and at least see the islands and coasts of the Mediterranean. They looked forward, likewise, with pleasure to a view of Madras, Colombo, and Bombay, to which they were to go in a sailing vessel.

But when the time came for leaving their father and the country of their birth, they did not feel *all* proud and happy; and after embarking, although their father was to go down the river with them for some distance, they turned their heads as they passed Garden Reach, and looked with moistened eyes at what seemed from that point of view a true City of Palaces. When their father finally bade them farewell, the two boys remained for some time in their cabin with their mother, who was very sad; and when she obliged them to go upon deck for amusement, they found that the whole scene had changed. The city had vanished, with its groves, and palaces, and shipping; and here there were only low and naked banks, with dark muddy waters between, and sometimes broken masts slanting up from the surface, to show where some unfortunate vessel had perished in the most dangerous navigation in the world.

It was a tedious voyage down the Hoogly, and everybody seemed anxious to get safely out to sea; and when they were at last fairly at the mouth of the river, and looked back to bid farewell to the land, the two boys thought to themselves that they had never beheld so dull, lifeless, and uninteresting a scene. The low marshy island of Saugor seemed a proper outpost of the long lines of swamp and jungle from which they had emerged, and the young travellers listened with a shudder to the stories they heard on all sides of the tigers which inhabit its dismal woods.

For the first day or two after leaving the river, they were too sick to see or even think of anything; and for some time after they were well enough to go upon deck, they were confined to the cabin by a storm. The convulsive rolling of the ship, the groaning of her timbers, the roar of the wind, the rattling of the rigging, and the shouts of the seamen, all terrified and confounded them; and perhaps they wished at the moment that they were still at Calcutta.

"Mamma," said they, "this is worse than the Ganges!" But their mother was still too unwell to comfort them, otherwise than by pressing them in her arms, as if there they were safe from the storm. But the wind at length moderated; and one day when all three went upon deck, they were delighted to see a long level line of coast before them.

"Is that Madras, Mr Stanley?" cried Alfred, addressing an elderly gentleman, a friend of his father, who had undertaken to protect the party during their journey to England.

"Yes, my dear," said he. "We shall soon come to anchor in the roads."

"But what is that!" cried Charles in his turn —"that black man walking towards us on the sea? He has not even hold of a buffalo's tail!"

"That is a catamaran Jack. You cannot see his boat, which is a mere raft formed of three small logs lashed together, for it is level with the sea, and sometimes under it. Now you can see it springing over the waves, something like the sole of a sharp-pointed shoe; and now "——

"Oh he is gone! he is lost!"

"He is overboard sure enough; but if not laid hold of by a shark, Jack will take care of himself;" and in another minute he was indeed seen rising from the sea, standing once more on his catamaran, and paddling away as if nothing had happened.

They were now coming to anchor, surrounded by vessels of all builds and countries; but the boys could not keep their eyes off the catamaran man, who presently reached their vessel, clambered up the sides like a monkey, and sprang upon deck. He was of a small slight figure, and wore no clothes but a cloth round his middle, and a sugar-loaf cap of palmyra leaf.

"What does he want?" asked Charles, as he gazed on their strange visitor; and all the other passengers, and even the captain and officers of the ship, seemed to share his curiosity, for they gathered round him, and watched with interest, as, after a low salaam to the captain, he took off his palmyra cap and extricated some letters from between the outer and inner lining.

"Charles," said Alfred, "he is a dâk carrier of the sea!" and the two boys laughed heartily at the idea. They then looked towards the land, which was the next object of interest, and Mr Stanley explained that it was Fort St George and the sea front of Black Town that were opposite them. The effect was very fine; for long ranges of buildings, with white verandas, stretched along the beach; and beautiful trees, especially the graceful cocoa-nut, filled up the picture.

Several other boats now approached the ship, very different from the catamaran, but quite as curious. They were high out of the water at bow and stern, and looked too solid and unwieldy for so short a trip, and for a cargo of nothing more than fresh bread, eggs, butter, plantains, and newspapers. These were Massoulah boats; and among them there was one painted more gaily than the rest, called an "accommodation-boat," in which passengers might land if they chose. Much to Alfred's satisfaction, it was arranged that he and Mr Stanley should go on shore for some hours; but Charles being too young, as they said, to be taken "through the surf," his mother remained with him on board. Alfred could see a white line on the water, near the shore, but no great surf to be afraid of; and he kissed his hand gaily to his mother and brother as the accommodation-boat pushed off from the ship, and the wild-looking rowers began a dismal chant, keeping time with their oars.

As they got nearer and nearer the white line on the water, a roaring voice came from it that mingled with the black men's song; and Alfred saw that it was a range of breakers, whirling, bursting, and dashing, which completely hid the land from their view. He began to be afraid, and what was worse, the very rowers showed symptoms of fear too. They turned their black flashing eyes from the boat to the surf, from the surf to the passengers, and from the passengers to one another; and their song became louder, and shriller, and wilder, till, as they actually reached the breakers, it grew into an unearthly yell. The boat rose upon the top of an enormous wave; and then, by a sudden exertion of strength, the men plunged her into the trough beyond to escape the burst; but with only partial success, for all on board were drenched with the spray.

The song now sank into its ordinary tone, and Alfred had nearly recovered from his terror, when a wild yell broke anew from the rowers, and they found themselves on the top of another wave, to be plunged once more into the abyss, and covered once more with the shower. Yet a third time they came through the same peril; and then, to the boy's unspeakable relief, they were thrown high upon the beach.

"Why, you are quite a brave fellow!" said Mr Stanley, who had remained perfectly calm. "You did not utter a word the whole time."

"I was too much frightened to speak," replied Alfred honestly. "But was there not really danger?"

"None at all in fine weather like this, or you would not have been here. These clumsy Massoulah boats are contrived on purpose for the service, and the terror of the rowers was all a pretence. But here we are in Madras. What do you think of it?" Alfred prudently suspended his opinion; but in the course of the day declared that it was not by any means so fine a city as Calcutta. "There is no glass," he remarked, "in any of the windows that I can see, and no punkah in any of the drawing-rooms. Then look at these miserable horses and ugly vehicles—the natives are better off with their bullocks." On going to the Black Town, they found the houses built of mud, and none of the windows (which are here only little square holes) towards the street. The doors were not higher than a man's shoulder, and the low passages from which they opened, leading from the street, were the reception-room, where the master conversed with his guests. As for the lower classes, they lived in hovels not more than three feet high; and when they wished to move to another habitation, they merely carried off their roof, leaving the walls to be washed away by the next rains. Yet in this Black Town, it is said, there are half a million of people; and the noise they make in speaking, scolding, singing, squibbing, crackering, and tom-toming morning, noon, and night, is astounding.

When returning on board, Alfred was not much better reconciled to the surf. The great art of the rowers was to catch the moment for passing each wave when it was still unbroken; but at length they came through them all, and were again on the smooth and beautiful sea. He had great pleasure in telling his mother of all he had seen, and little Charles regarded his brother as a perfect hero.

There was not much to interest them while running down the Coromandel coast, the land was so low and naked, with only here and there a few huts, or a pagoda, or a cocoa-nut or palmyra-tree; but the weather was fine, the sea smooth, and the native craft, with their striped latteen sails, gliding along, gave life to the picture. When the beautiful island of Ceylon came in view, called Serendib in the "Arabian Nights," the scene was not much improved in variety; for on this side it differs little from the continental coast, except in being covered with trees. But at last the strange mountain called Adam's Peak was seen rising inland, almost like a human figure wrapped in a cloak; and soon after the ship was within a few miles of the fort of Colombo. Here a number of small vessels crowded round them like flies; and Alfred and Charles speculated deeply on the difference between them and the Madras boats. The Cingalese boats were small, sharp, and frail, and were carried like the wind itself along the sea by a single enormous sail.

"Isn't it curious," said Alfred, who was growing learned in nautical matters, "that they do not tumble over?"

"They would certainly capsize," replied Mr Stanley, " were it not for a contrivance which you will see when they come nearer, called an *outrigger*. This is a log of wood floating on the water, which is connected with the boat by a slight spar; and provided with this simple machine, the poor little vessel lives in a sea that would sorely try a much more powerful one."

When they came close to the side, Alfred looked at these outriggers with great curiosity; but his attention was speedily attracted by the fruit, fish, and bread which they brought. His mother bought some fine pine-apples for three-halfpence each.

As the ship, being large, did not approach the land nearer than a mile, very few of the passengers landed excepting those whose destination was Ceylon; and although there was no surf to be dreaded on this coast, Alfred was very well contented to remain on board.

The weather still continuing fine, the run along the Malabar coast to Bombay was very pleasant, and diversified with views of the dim mountains of the interior. The island of Bombay does not contain above half the population of Madras; but there are many ships of all nations continually arriving and departing, and crowds of coasting vessels hovering about. The fort or garrison has fifteen thousand inhabitants to its own share; and the travellers thought the effect of a long line of bungalows on the esplanade, extending for nearly a mile along the sea-shore, extremely pleasing. They are of wood, with trelliswork of bamboo, and are thatched with palmyra leaves, lined inside with coloured cloth, ceiled with white calico, and surrounded with canvas like a tent. They have almost all gardens; and the railings round the compound are hung with a rich drapery of creeping plants, including the passion-flower.

"Oh how I should like to live in one of these beautiful bungalows!" said Alfred. "I should remain in it all the year round, without ever wishing to enter the town."

"Then you would be a hermit," said Mr Stanley smiling; "for in the middle of May everybody runs away from the coming rains, and the dwellings themselves vanish. Nothing is seen on the esplanade but ruined shrubberies, broken flower-pots, torn paper-hangings, straw, and refuse."

"And who clears all that away?"

"The rains appear to melt everything into the ground; and in the course of a single week after they begin to fall, a beautiful green-sward clothes the esplanade like a carpet. By the middle of June all is rich and beautiful; and before October the city of villas has risen anew, with its shrubs and gardens, as if called by enchantment out of the ground."

Within the fort or European town the travellers found at this season but few English, excepting those who required to attend to their official or other business. But Alfred was glad to see again the punkahs in full swing, even in the church; and there indeed they had a strange effect, hanging in rows all the length of the nave, and flapping backwards and forwards by unseen agency, the cords being pulled by natives outside the walls. Between the fort and the country is the native town; and there the boys were much amused with the busy scene presented by the bazaar, and its extraordinary variety of colours, dresses, complexions, and occupations.

It was a week before the steamer for Suez was ready to sail; but at length our travellers were once more on the sea; and in eight or ten days they made the point of Aden, and in due time anchored in Back Bay, while guns, rockets, and signal lanterns were exchanged between the ship and the shore. Barren rocks, a sandy beach, with a few buildings, and mountains beyond like masses of cinders, these were all the prospects presented; and there being no means of getting to the native town but by walking several miles along the beach, Alfred and Charles were obliged to content themselves on board, watching the men called *seedies* employed in transhipping the coal, who kept screaming their wild songs, and dancing and clapping their hands, while they were at work, in a most extraordinary manner. The real labour, however, even without this addition, was too hard; for Mr Stanley told them that every hundred tons of coals delivered cost the life of a man, who lay down after his task, and never rose again.

Before reaching Suez, the boys were fairly sick of the Red Sea, so far as its scenery was concerned, which they found very uninteresting, although their mother turned their travels to profit by pointing out what is supposed to be the place where the Israelites crossed, and some hills in the distance that bore the well-known names of Sinai and Horeb. Suez was, if possible, worse than Aden. "The buildings," as a traveller says, " remind one of houses built by children with torn and dirty cards;" and they rise out of bare sand, for the place is on the borders of the desert.

It was not without some alarm as well as curiosity that the boys set out to cross the desert with a caravan of camels, horses, and donkeys; but the jolting of the rude vans over the stony parts of the road soon put everything out of their heads but a feeling of discomfort. In this journey of eighty miles to Grand Cairo, they encountered a single tree and some stunted bushes, with here and there the skeleton of a camel lying on the sand. The stations for rest and refreshment were the only other objects of interest; but these, although improved since then, were not half so comfortable as a stable in England. On the third day Charles could not help crying; and even Alfred, whose travels, he thought, had by this time made him quite a man, was a good deal disheartened.

"When do you think, mamma," said he in a low dispirited voice, "we shall come to the end of this sea of sand and stones, which has no other inhabitants than bugs and fleas?"

"I think I saw something like a tower already," replied his mamma; "but I am so cramped up in this miserable box that I cannot turn my head."

"Courage!" cried Mr Stanley, who was on a dromedary by their side: "there are the minarets of Grand Cairo—there are the Pyramids of Egypt!" And making an effort to look, all the travellers in the van saw sure enough before them, at a distance of some eight or ten miles, those objects which every one has heard of.

As the Pyramids were seen closer, Alfred continued to gaze on them in silence, and with great gravity. At last he said—"Mamma, I always thought the Pyramids were as large as hills; but these appear very little."

"You do well to say appear," replied his mamma; "for they are in reality stupendous. When we are in London, I shall take you to a very large square called Lincoln's-Inn-Fields, and if you imagine a building the size of that square raised into a pyramid a hundred and nineteen feet higher than St Paul's, you will obtain some idea of the Great Pyramid."

"Then why do they look so small?"

"It is partly, I think," said Mr Stanley, "owing to the squatness, if so mean an expression is permitted, of their shape; but principally because there is no object with the size of which we are acquainted sufficiently near them to serve for comparison. If you were close enough to see human beings crawling up their sides, they would resemble insects; and thus you would come to form an adequate idea of the grandeur of the Pyramid." Alfred afterwards saw these extraordinary objects from the terrace of the Citadel, and when descending the Nile; and before he lost sight of them, he had, without knowing it himself, corrected his first impressions.

The amusements the boys enjoyed most in Grand Cairo were the bazaars. Each article of trade had its separate bazaar; and the places devoted to articles of dress were more especially splendid, and sometimes so crowded, that it was difficult to pass through them on their small Egyptian donkeys. The baths they did not like so well; and indeed Alfred was so long a time under the operation, and was so thoroughly shampooed, soaped, dashed with hot and cold water, pasted with clay, and rubbed with horsehair gloves and calcined stone, that the end of it was, he fell asleep in the hands of his bather. The great square of Esbequieh was a pleasant lounge, with its lakes and wooded avenues, its itinerant coffee and sherbet shops, its juggling and dancing exhibitions, and, above all, its variety of company, Asiatic and European, in dresses of every shape and hue. But after all, the city looked to best advantage from the lofty walls of the Citadel; with its mosques, minarets, fountains, palaces, and harems; the aqueduct and its graceful arches; the garden of El Rhoda; the ruins of Old Cairo; the groves of sycamore and palm-trees; the beautiful lakes; the Nile with its picturesque boats; and beyond all, the Pyramids and the Lybian Desert.

Leaving Grand Cairo, they embarked upon the Nile at the port of Boulac, about two miles distant; and gliding through its ravines, took the Mahmoudieh Canal at Atfé for Alexandria. The construction of this canal, Mr Stanley told Alfred, was the cause of dreadful misery and loss of life; the labourers being brought by compulsion, and provided neither with proper tools nor proper food—no fewer than twenty thousand of them dying from the effects of famine and fatigue! The villages on the banks were mere clusters of square or round mud huts, looking very unlike the abiding-places of human beings; although when they reached the neighbourhood of Alexandria there were plenty of white villas enclosed in gardens. Many of the boats they passed were plastered with mud, like the peasants' houses, with grass growing on their sides. They disembarked at some little distance from the town, and were gratified by passing close to Pompey's Pillar, which is said to be one of the finest columns in the world. The obelisk called Cleopatra's Needle was not far distant. It was lucky that they had seen something; for Alexandria itself is on one side a cluster of modern offices, and on the other a heap of ancient but uninteresting ruins. Narrow lanes and alleys, destitute of air and light, and full of dirt and misery, sufficiently account for this place being chosen as its head-quarters by the plague.

The travellers, upon the whole, were not sorry to leave Egypt; and when embarked upon the Mediterranean, in the steamer which was to convey them *home*, you may be sure they were all busy with their own thoughts, and hopes, and memories. Having come from a plague country, they were not permitted to visit any part of the island of Malta but a building near the shore called the lazaretto; and even here, although the place resembled a bazaar, they were separated from the sellers by a rail. The gold and silver money that was paid for fruit, ices, and ornaments of various kinds, was passed through vinegar and water, and the jewellers presented their articles to their customers with a pair of tongs. Charles began to feel some alarm at these precautions; and when Alfred asked him in a whisper whether they had really the plague, he referred him for an answer to his mother.

After leaving Malta, they had a fine view of Algiers, then of Gibraltar, and then of the shores of Spain and Portugal; but all these were forgotten when the coast of England rose gradually above the edge of the sea. The two children with cries of joy dragged their mother out of the cabin to see it; but they were suddenly silent when they found that tears were mingled with her smiles and kisses. Even the old and sedate Mr Stanley was moved; and his voice quivered as he said to the youthful travellers, seeming to suggest some proud comparison with the many lands they had seen—"There, boys, is the country of your ancestors! There is free, happy, beautiful OLD ENGLAND!"

THE END

www.ingramcontent.com/pod-product-compliance
Lightning Source LLC
Chambersburg PA
CBHW032150160426
43197CB00008B/849